D1806112

GREAT COOKING MADE EASY

VERSATILE VEGETABLES

Better Homes and Gardens
TRADEMARK

TREASURE PRESS

BETTER HOMES AND GARDENS BOOKS

Editor Gerald M. Knox
Art Director Ernest Shelton
Managing Editor David A. Kirchner
Project Editors James D. Blume, Marsha Jahns
Project Managers Liz Anderson, Jennifer Speer Ramundt, Angela K. Renkoski

Vegetables (American edition)
Editor Maureen Powers
Project Manager Mary Helen Schiltz
Graphic Designer Harijs Priekulis
Electronic Text Processor Donna Russell
Photographers Michael Jensen, Sean Fitzgerald
Food Stylists Suzanne Finley, Carol Grones, Dianna Nolin, Janet Herwig
Contributing Writer Sandra Mosley

Versatile Vegetables (British edition)
Project Managers Liz Anderson, Angela K. Renkoski
Assistant Art Director Harijs Priekulis
Contributing Project Editors Irena Chalmers Books, Inc., and associates: Jean Atcheson,
Irena Chalmers, Ann Chase, Mary Dauman, Cathy Garvey,
Mary Goodbody, Terri Griffing, Margaret Homberg, Kathryn Knapp,
Stephanie Lyness, Susan Anderson Nabel, Victoria Proctor,
Elizabeth Wheeler
Electronic Text Processors Alice Bauman, Kathy Benz, Paula Forest, Vicki Howell,
Mary Mathews, Joyce Wasson

This edition first published in Great Britain in 1989 by:

Treasure Press
Michelin House
81 Fulham Road
London, SW3 6RB

© Copyright 1987, 1989 by Meredith Corporation, Des Moines,
Iowa, U.S.A. All rights reserved. No part of this publication may be
reproduced, stored in a retrieval system, or transmitted in any form or
by any means, electronic, mechanical, photocopying, recording, or
otherwise, without the prior permission of the Copyright owner.

Original edition published by Meredith Corporation in the
United States of America.

BETTER HOMES AND GARDENS is a registered trademark in
Canada, New Zealand, South Africa, and other countries.

ISBN 1 85051 430 5

Produced by Mandarin Offset
Printed and bound in Hong Kong

Vegetables, glorious vegetables! Today's interest in health, nutrition, dieting, and eating light is fast making vegetables a favourite dish at any meal—and sometimes they're the *only* dish!

Here you'll rediscover old favourites and get acquainted with an assortment of new and unusual vegetable-garden goodies. Look for quick-to-make recipes or upmarket, elegant dishes. When you don't need a recipe, easy-to-read charts with simple-to-follow directions help you cook fresh vegetables to perfection.

From soup to dessert, bread to salad, side dish to main dish, vegetables take a prominent place in the hearts of food lovers. One sample from *Versatile Vegetables,* and we're sure you'll want to give your own "taste-amony" to these recipes that make the most of nature's abundant harvest.

Contents

Vegetables That Go Crunch

First slice 'em and dice 'em. Then, munch 'em and crunch 'em.

Uncooked vegetables will fit right in with your life-style. Light, fresh, and quick-to-make, these salads and appetisers are ideal for busy people looking for healthy, delicious vegetables.

Appetising Antipasto

Appetising Antipasto

Whet appetites before dinner or at a party with a beautifully arranged hors d'oeuvre dish of fresh vegetables, meats, and cheeses.

8 ounces (225g) broccoli *or* cauliflower
2 small yellow crookneck squash *or* courgettes
2 medium carrots
2 small tomatoes
4½ ounces (125g) stoned ripe olives
2¾ fluid ounces (70ml) olive oil *or* salad oil
2 fluid ounces (55ml) white wine vinegar
1 tablespoon snipped parsley
1 tablespoon lemon juice
2 teaspoons French mustard
½ teaspoon dried basil *or* marjoram, crushed
⅛ teaspoon pepper
Leaf lettuce
4 ounces (110g) thinly sliced salami
4 ounces (110g) provolone *or* mozzarella cheese, cut into sticks
Melba toast rounds *or* French bread (optional)

Wash all vegetables thoroughly. Cut broccoli or cauliflower into florets (see photo 1). Thinly slice crookneck squash or courgettes (see photo 2). Cut carrots into julienne strips (see photo 3). Cut tomatoes into thin wedges (see photo 4). In a large bowl combine prepared vegetables and olives.

For marinade, in a screw-top jar combine olive oil or salad oil, vinegar, parsley, lemon juice, mustard, basil or marjoram, and pepper. Cover and shake well (see photo 5). Pour marinade over vegetable mixture; toss to coat. Cover and chill 2 to 24 hours, stirring occasionally to distribute marinade.

Line a serving dish with leaf lettuce. Using a slotted spoon, transfer vegetables and olives to the. Fold salami slices in half; arrange salami and cheese sticks on the dish. Serve with Melba toast or French bread, if desired. Makes 6 to 8 servings.

1 Trim the leaves from the broccoli and wash it under cold running water. Cut off just the florets with a sharp knife, as shown. Reserve the stalks to use later in soups or casseroles.

2 To slice squash, hold the vegetable firmly against the cutting board. Place a thin, sharp knife atop the vegetable at a 45-degree angle about ¼ inch (.5cm) from the edge. Then cut down and out.

3 To make julienne strips, cut the carrots in half crosswise, then in half lengthwise. Continue cutting the carrots lengthwise to create long, thin strips, as shown.

4 For neat, thin tomato wedges, cut the tomato in half with a serrated knife and remove the core. Then slice the tomato into wedges using a light back-and-forth motion.

5 An easy way to thoroughly mix ingredients is to place them in a jar with a screw-top lid. Tighten the lid on the jar and shake vigorously to combine the ingredients.

Crunchy Jicama Salad

Jicama (HEE kuh muh) is often used in southwestern American cooking. (See page 121 for an illustration.)

5⅓	ounces (165g) cubed jicama
3	ounces (75g) sliced celery
2	ounces (50g) chopped onion
2	tablespoons chopped sweet pickled cucumber
3	ounces (75g) mayonnaise
1	teaspoon caster sugar
1	teaspoon celery seed
1	teaspoon prepared mustard
1	hard-boiled egg, coarsely chopped
	Lettuce leaves
1	hard-boiled egg, sliced (optional)

In a medium bowl combine jicama, celery, onion, and sweet pickled cucumber.

For dressing, in a small bowl combine mayonnaise, sugar, celery seed, mustard, and ¼ teaspoon *salt*. Add dressing to jicama mixture; toss to coat. Gently fold in chopped egg. Cover and chill. Spoon salad into lettuce-lined serving bowl. Garnish with hard-boiled egg slices, if desired. Makes 4 servings.

Creamy Curry-Vegetable Salad

Use either daikon (DIKE un), mooli, or parsnips in this simple, yet sophisticated salad. See pages 120–121 for more helpful hints on using unusual vegetables.

1	small courgette, cut into julienne strips (see photo 3, page 9)
3	ounces (75g) julienne strips daikon, mooli, *or* parsnip (see photo 3, page 9)
3	ounces (75g) sliced celery (see photo 2, page 8)
2½	ounces (60g) cashews *or* peanuts
2¾	ounces (70g) natural yogurt
2	tablespoons orange juice
½	teaspoon curry powder

In a bowl combine courgette, daikon, mooli, or parsnip, celery, and cashews or peanuts.

For dressing, in a small bowl combine natural yogurt, orange juice, and curry powder. Pour dressing over courgette mixture; toss to coat. Makes 4 servings.

The Cutting Edge

Cubing: Use a chef's knife to cut strips of jicama about 1cm wide. Then cut crosswise to make cubes ½ inch (1cm) on all sides.

Dicing: Cut the same as for cubing, but make the pieces smaller. Ingredients that are diced are cut into ⅛- to ¼-inch (3mm-.5cm) pieces.

Chopping: Cut foods into irregularly shaped pieces about the size of peas using a knife, chopper, blender, or food processor.

Mincing: Use a utility knife or paring knife to cut the food (usually garlic cloves) into very tiny, irregularly shaped pieces.

Cucumber-Spinach Dip with Crudités

Crudités (kroo dee tay) is just a fancy way of saying a selection of raw sliced vegetables.

4 ounces (110g) natural yogurt
4 ounces (110g) soured cream
¼ teaspoon salt
¼ teaspoon dried dill
 Dash bottled hot pepper sauce
3 ounces (75g) finely chopped, seeded cucumber
1 ounce (25g) finely chopped spinach *or* lettuce
 Assorted vegetable dippers*

In a small bowl combine yogurt, soured cream, salt, dill, and hot pepper sauce. Stir in cucumber and spinach or lettuce. Cover and chill 2 to 24 hours.

Prepare assorted vegetable dippers or crudités. Seal vegetables in a clear polythene bag or air-tight container and chill until serving time.

Place dip in the centre of a serving plate. Arrange vegetable dippers around dip. Makes about 12 ounces (350g) dip (24 servings).

*Choose from broccoli or cauliflower florets (see photo 1, page 8), courgette or yellow crookneck squash slices (see photo 2, page 8), julienne carrots (see photo 3, page 9), cherry tomatoes or tomato wedges (see photo 4, page 9), spring onions, fresh mushrooms, and green pepper squares or strips.

Tomato-Mushroom Salad

Tarragon lends a subtle herb flavour.

3 medium tomatoes *or* 24 cherry tomatoes
3 ounces (75g) sliced fresh mushrooms
2 spring onions, thinly sliced
3 tablespoons olive oil *or* salad oil
3 tablespoons vinegar
1 tablespoon water
1 teaspoon caster sugar
¼ teaspoon dried tarragon, crushed
 Dash bottled hot pepper sauce
8 ounces (225g) torn lettuce, romaine, *or* spinach

Cut tomatoes into thin wedges (see photo 4, page 9). (Or, cut cherry tomatoes in half.) In a medium bowl combine tomatoes, mushrooms, and spring onions.

For marinade, in a screw-top jar combine olive oil or salad oil, vinegar, water, sugar, tarragon, and hot pepper sauce. Cover and shake well (see photo 5, page 9). Pour marinade over vegetable mixture; toss gently to coat. Cover and chill 2 to 24 hours, stirring occasionally to distribute marinade.

Place lettuce, romaine, or spinach in a salad bowl. Add marinated vegetable mixture. Toss to coat. Makes 6 servings.

The Best Of Boiling

Simple doesn't mean boring—it means sensational!

Each delectable side dish starts with boiling water and fresh vegetables. After cooking to perfect crisp-tenderness, we jazz up these vegetables with a flash of exciting flavour.

And to think, it's all as easy as boiling water.

Sesame Broccoli

Sesame Broccoli

"Open sesame!" Ali Baba used that phrase to open a secret cave containing valuable treasures. We use sesame seed to open your taste buds to this gem of a recipe.

1 **pound (450g) broccoli, cut into spears,**
   or **10 ounces (275g) frozen broccoli**
   spears
2 **tablespoons butter** *or* **margarine**
1 **tablespoon sesame seed**
2 **tablespoons diced pimento**
1 **tablespoon lemon juice**
   Dash pepper
   Lemon slices (optional)

In a medium saucepan bring 8 fluid ounces (220ml) lightly salted water to boiling. Add broccoli (see photo 1). Return to boiling; reduce heat. Cook, covered, for 11 to 12 minutes or until broccoli is crisp-tender (see photo 2). (*Or,* cook frozen broccoli according to package directions.) Drain broccoli (see photo 3). Return broccoli to saucepan.

Meanwhile, in a small frying pan melt butter or margarine. Add sesame seed; cook and stir until seeds are light brown (see photo 4). Remove from heat. Add pimento, lemon juice, and pepper. Pour sesame mixture over broccoli; stir to coat. Transfer to a serving bowl. Garnish with lemon slices, if desired. Makes 4 servings.

1 Lower the broccoli into the saucepan with tongs or a large spoon to avoid splashing boiling water or burning your hands with the steam.

2 Pierce the stalk or toughest part of the vegetable to test if it's tender. When a fork will just go into the food easily, the vegetable is *crisp-tender* (that is, tender but still crisp).

3 Place a colander in the sink, then pour the broccoli into the colander. Give the colander a few firm shakes to drain the water from the broccoli.

4 Stir the sesame seeds constantly with a wooden spoon while you are browning them in the hot butter or margarine. When the seeds are light brown, remove the pan from the heat immediately.

Crumb-Capped French Beans

½ pound (225g) French beans *or* 10 ounces (275g) frozen cut French beans
½ ounce (10g) seasoned croutons
1 tablespoon butter *or* margarine, melted

Wash fresh French beans; remove ends and strings. Cut beans into 1-inch (2.5cm) pieces. In a medium saucepan bring about 4 fluid ounces (110ml) lightly salted water to boiling. Add French beans (see photo 1, page 14). Return to boiling; reduce heat. Cook, covered, for 20 to 25 minutes or until crisp-tender (see photo 2, page 15). (*Or,* cook frozen beans according to packet directions.) Drain beans (see photo 3, page 15).

Meanwhile, crush croutons; stir together crouton crumbs and melted butter or margarine. Transfer beans to a serving bowl. Sprinkle crumb mixture atop beans. Makes 4 servings.

Glazed Onions

16 ounces (450g) pearl onions or frozen small whole onions
2 tablespoons butter *or* margarine
2 tablespoons soft brown sugar
2 ounces (50g) chopped green *or* sweet red pepper

In a medium saucepan bring about 4 fluid ounces (110ml) lightly salted water to boiling; add *unpeeled* onions (see photo 1, page 14). Return to boiling; reduce heat. Cook, covered, about 10 minutes or until just tender (see photo 2, page 15). (*Or,* cook frozen onions according to packet directions.) Drain onions (see photo 3, page 15). Cool pearl onions slightly; trim ends and remove skin.

In the same saucepan stir butter or margarine, brown sugar, and 1 tablespoon *water.* Cook and stir until combined. Add onions and green or red pepper. Simmer, uncovered, until onions are glazed, stirring occasionally. Serves 4.

Prawn-Stuffed Artichokes

The art of eating an artichoke is all in your fingers. Pull off a leaf and dunk it into the creamy prawn dip. Pull the leaf through your teeth, eating only the tender flesh, then discard the remainder of the leaf. Now you're ready for another one.

2 medium artichokes (about 8 ounces [225g] each)
Lemon juice
4 ounces (110g) frozen cooked prawns
4 ounces (110g) soured cream
4 ounces (110g) natural yogurt
1 tablespoon snipped parsley
1 tablespoon thinly sliced spring onion
¼ teaspoon dried tarragon, crushed
Dash bottled hot pepper sauce

Wash artichokes, trim stems, and remove loose outer leaves. Cut off 1 inch (2.5cm) of the tops. Snip off sharp leaf tips. Brush cut edges of leaves with lemon juice.

In a covered casserole bring a large amount (about 3 inches [7.5cm]) lightly salted water to boiling. Add artichokes (see photo 1, page 14). Return to boiling; reduce heat. Cook, covered, for 20 to 25 minutes or until a leaf pulls out easily. Using tongs, remove artichokes from casserole. Invert to drain; cool. Spread leaves apart. Pull out centre leaves and scrape out choke with a spoon; discard (see tip, page 17). Cover artichokes and chill.

Meanwhile, thaw, drain, and chop prawns. In a small bowl combine prawns, soured cream, yogurt, parsley, spring onion, tarragon, and hot pepper sauce. Cover and chill.

Spoon *half* of the prawn-soured-cream mixture into the centre of each artichoke. Makes 2 main-dish servings.

Orange Carrots And Sprouts

½ **pound (225g) brussels sprouts *or* 10 ounces (275g) frozen brussels sprouts**
4 **ounces (110g) thinly sliced carrots (3 medium)**
1 **tablespoon butter *or* margarine**
2 **tablespoons orange juice**
1 **teaspoon honey**
⅛ **teaspoon ground ginger**
2 **tablespoons coarsely chopped cashews *or* peanuts**

Cut large brussels sprouts in half. In a medium saucepan bring about 4 fluid ounces (110ml) lightly salted water to boiling. Add brussels sprouts and carrots (see photo 1, page 14). Return to boiling; reduce heat. Cook, covered, for 10 to 15 minutes or until crisp-tender (see photo 2, page 15). Drain vegetables (see photo 3, page 15). Return vegetables to the saucepan.

Meanwhile, in a small saucepan melt butter or margarine. Add orange juice, honey, and ginger. Bring to boiling. Pour over vegetables; stir gently to coat. Transfer to a serving bowl. Sprinkle with cashews or peanuts. Serves 4.

Creamy Chayote

Chayote (chah YOTE ee) is a light green, pear-shape squash with a delicate flavour.

¾ **pound (350g) chopped, peeled, seeded chayote**
4 **ounces (110g) natural yogurt**
2 **tablespoons snipped parsley *or* 1 tablespoon snipped cilantro**
½ **teaspoon caster sugar**
 Several dashes paprika
 Dash pepper
 Lettuce leaves (optional)
1½ **ounces (40g) chopped peanuts**

In a medium saucepan bring about 4 fluid ounces (110ml) lightly salted water to boiling. Add chayote (see photo 1, page 14). Return to boiling; reduce heat. Cook, covered, about 5 minutes or until crisp-tender (see photo 2, page 15). Drain chayote (see photo 3, page 15). Chill at least 1 hour.

In a small bowl combine yogurt, parsley or cilantro, sugar, paprika, and pepper. Add chayote; toss gently. Spoon into lettuce-lined bowl, if desired. Sprinkle with peanuts. Makes 4 servings.

The Inside Scoop on Artichokes

Preparing and eating an artichoke aren't perplexing when you know what's inside.
●**Centre leaves:** Purplish, prickly leaves in the middle of the artichoke. Remove these before you stuff a whole artichoke.
●**Choke:** Fuzzy, thistle portion located just below the center leaves. Scrape this out with a small, strong spoon and discard.
●**Heart:** Succulent, nut-flavoured base just below the choke. Cut into bite-size pieces and dip into butter or sauce.

Taters and Toppers

If your meal-time luck is at a draw, here's an ace up your sleeve. These baked potatoes and tempting toppers will make your meal a winning hand.

Whether you're looking for satisfying South-of-the-Border (Mexican-style) Taters or intriguing Curried Chicken in Potatoes, these vegetables are worth betting on.

Potatoes with Prawn Creole Topper

Potatoes with Prawn Creole Topper

4 **medium baking potatoes (6 to 8 ounces [175 to 225g] each)***

½ **pound (225g) fresh *or* frozen peeled and deveined prawns**

29 **ounces (800g) tinned tomatoes, cut up**

2 **ounces (50g) chopped onion**

2 **ounces (50g) chopped celery *or* green pepper**

1 **tablespoon snipped parsley**

1 **clove garlic, minced**

1 **ounce (25g) cornflour**

⅛ **teaspoon ground red pepper**

Scrub potatoes thoroughly (see photo 1). For soft skins, rub potatoes with lard.

Prick potatoes with a fork (see photo 2). Bake potatoes in a 425°F (220°C) gas mark 7 oven for 40 to 60 minutes or until done (see photo 3). (*Or*, bake in a 350°F [180°C] gas mark 4 oven for 70 to 80 minutes.) Roll each potato gently under your hand. Cut a crisscross in the top of each potato with a knife. Press ends and push up (see photo 4).

Meanwhile, thaw prawns, if frozen; drain. In a medium saucepan combine *undrained* tomatoes, onion, celery or green pepper, parsley, garlic, cornflour, and red pepper. Cook and stir until thickened and bubbly. Stir in prawns. Cover and cook 3 to 5 minutes more or until prawns are cooked. Spoon prawn mixture over potatoes. Makes 4 main-dish servings.

***Note:** To foil-bake potatoes, prepare as above, *except* omit rubbing with lard. Prick potatoes with a fork (see photo 2). Wrap each potato in foil. Continue as directed above.

1 Scrub the potatoes gently but thoroughly with a vegetable brush under running water. Remove sprouts. Then pat the potatoes dry with kitchen paper.

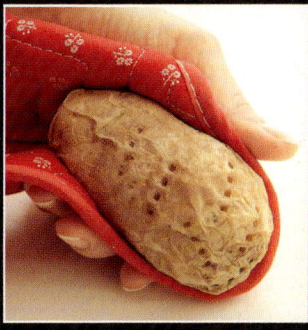

2 Prick the skin of the potatoes several times with the prongs of a fork. This gives the steam a place to escape, preventing the potatoes from bursting.

3 To see if the potatoes are ready, squeeze them with an oven glove, as shown, or pierce them with a fork. When they feel soft, the potatoes are done.

4 To fluff a baked potato, gently roll the potato under your hand on the work surface. Cut a crisscross in the top. Then, press in and up on the two ends of the potato, as shown.

Micro-Baked Potatoes

Scrub 4 medium baking potatoes (6 to 8 ounces [175 to 225g] each). Prick with a fork. In a microwave oven arrange potatoes on microwave-safe kitchen papers, leaving at least 1 inch (2.5cm) between potatoes. Micro-cook, uncovered, on 100% power (HIGH) for 13 to 16 minutes or till done. (Or, allow 5 to 7 minutes for 1 potato; 7 to 9 minutes for 2 potatoes.) Halfway through, turn potatoes over and rearrange. Let stand for 5 minutes.

Try-a-Topper Taters

1 **medium baking potato (6 to 8 ounces [175 to 225g] each)**
3 **ounces (75g) soured cream dip with toasted onion *or* with bacon and horseradish sauce**

Scrub potato thoroughly (*see* photo 1, page 21). For soft skin, rub potato with lard. Prick potato with a fork (*see* photo 2, page 21). Bake potato in a 425°F (220°C) gas mark 7 oven for 40 to 60 minutes or until done (*see* photo 3, page 21). (*Or,* bake in a 350°F [180°C] gas mark 4 oven for 70 to 80 minutes.) Roll potato gently under your hand. Cut a crisscross in top with a knife. Press ends and push up (*see* photo 4, page 21). Spoon soured cream dip over potato. Makes 1 main-dish serving.

Greek Potato: Prepare potato as above, *except* substitute a mixture of 3 ounces (75g) *natural yogurt,* 2 tablespoons sliced *ripe olives,* and a pinch of dried *oregano* for the dip. Spoon over potato. Sprinkle with chopped tomato.

Garden Potato: Prepare potato as above, *except* substitute a mixture of 2 ounces (50g) *cottage cheese* and 1½ ounces (40g) grated *cheddar,* crumbled *feta,* or crumbled *blue cheese* (at room temperature) for the dip. Spoon over potato. Top with *alfalfa sprouts,* 1 tablespoon finely chopped *green pepper,* and 1 tablespoon finely chopped *radish.*

Low-Cal Potato: Prepare potato as above, *except* substitute *natural low-fat yogurt* for the dip. Sprinkle with snipped *chives.*

Cheesy Potato: Prepare potato as above, *except* substitute grated *cheddar, processed, Swiss,* or *Gouda cheese,* or crumbled *blue cheese* (at room temperature) for the dip.

Cream Cheese Potato: Prepare potato as above, *except* substitute *soft-style cream cheese* (thinned with milk, if desired) for the dip. Sprinkle with crumbled, crisp-cooked streaky *bacon* and sliced *spring onion* or snipped *chives.*

Mexican Cheese Potatoes

Make a meal out of one of these main-dish variations.

2 **medium baking potatoes (6 to 8 ounces [175 to 225g] each)**
15 **ounces (425g) taco sauce**
3 **ounces (75g) grated cheddar cheese**
  Taco chips (optional)

Scrub potatoes thoroughly (*see* photo 1, page 21). For soft skins, rub potatoes with lard. Prick potatoes with a fork (*see* photo 2, page 21). Bake potatoes in a 425°F (220°C) gas mark 7 oven for 40 to 60 minutes or until done (*see* photo 3, page 21). (*Or,* bake in a 350°F [180°C] gas mark 4 oven for 70 to 80 minutes.) Roll each potato gently under your hand. Cut a crisscross in the top with a knife. Press ends and push up (*see* photo 4, page 21).

Meanwhile, in a medium saucepan heat taco sauce. Spoon sauce over baked potatoes. Sprinkle potatoes with cheese. Serve with taco chips, if desired. Makes 2 main-dish servings.

Barbecue-Style Potatoes: Prepare potatoes as above, *except* omit the taco sauce and cheddar cheese. In a small saucepan heat 4 fluid ounces (110ml) *barbecue sauce* and 2 fluid ounces (55ml) *apple juice.* Add 2 *frankfurters,* thinly sliced; heat through. Spoon frankfurter mixture over baked potatoes. Sprinkle with 3 ounces (75g) grated *mozzarella or Gouda cheese.*

Meat and Potatoes: Prepare potatoes as above, *except* omit the taco sauce and cheese. In a medium saucepan combine 8 fluid ounces (220ml) *beef or chicken consommé* and 5 ounces (150g) cubed cooked *beef, chicken, or turkey.* Heat through. Spoon sauce over baked potatoes.

South-of-the-Border Taters

Bring home the taste of sunny Mexico tonight! One secret to these great baked potato creations is to have the toppings at room temperature so the potatoes stay piping hot.

1 **large tomato, peeled and finely chopped**
2 **tablespoons finely chopped onion**
1 **tablespoon finely chopped green pepper**
1 **tablespoon finely chopped tinned green chilli peppers *or* 2 teaspoons finely chopped jalapeño peppers**
1 **clove garlic, minced**
¼ **teaspoon salt**
6 **ounces (175g) guacamole**
4 **medium baking potatoes (6 to 8 ounces [175 to 225g] each)**

For sauce, in a medium bowl stir together tomato, onion, green pepper, chilli peppers or jalapeño peppers, garlic, and salt. Cover; let stand at room temperature for 2 hours.

Scrub potatoes thoroughly (see photo 1, page 21). For soft skins, rub potatoes with lard. Prick potatoes with a fork (see photo 2, page 21). Bake potatoes in a 425°F (220°C) gas mark 7 oven for 40 to 60 minutes or until done (see photo 3, page 21). (*Or,* bake potatoes in a 350°F [180°C] gas mark 4 oven for 70 to 80 minutes.) Roll each potato gently under your hand. Cut a crisscross in the top with a knife. Press ends and push up (see photo 4, page 21).

To serve, pass tomato-pepper sauce and guacamole with baked potatoes. Makes 4 servings.

Curried Chicken In Potatoes

3 **medium baking potatoes (6 to 8 ounces [175 to 225g] each)**
1 **tablespoon butter *or* margarine**
2 **ounces (50g) chopped green pepper *or* celery**
1 **tablespoon sliced spring onion**
1 **teaspoon curry powder**
6 **ounces (175g) cubed cooked chicken**
7½ **fluid ounces (205ml) cream of mushroom soup**

Scrub potatoes thoroughly (see photo 1, page 21). For soft skins, rub potatoes with lard. Prick potatoes with a fork (see photo 2, page 21). Bake potatoes in a 425°F (220°C) gas mark 7 oven for 40 to 60 minutes or until done (see photo 3, page 21). (*Or,* bake in a 350°F [180°C] gas mark 4 oven for 70 to 80 minutes.) Roll each potato gently under your hand. Cut a crisscross in the top with a knife. Press ends and push up (see photo 4, page 21).

Meanwhile, in a small saucepan melt butter or margarine. Add green pepper or celery, onion, and curry. Cook until vegetables are tender but not brown. Stir in chicken and soup. Heat through. Serve chicken mixture over potatoes. Makes 3 main-dish servings.

Attention Microwave Owners!

The microwave timings in this book were tested using countertop microwave ovens with 600 to 700 watts of cooking power. The cooking times are approximate because microwave ovens vary by manufacturer.

Scrumptious Soups

Come one, come all! Step right up for the most exciting selection of super-delicious soups ever!

Main attractions include classic French Onion Soup, simple hearty Jambalaya Soup, and elegant Celery-Spinach Soup. Whatever your pleasure—simple or sophisticated, conventional or classic—it's right here.

French Onion Soup

French Onion Soup

Smothered with mounds of melted cheese, this delicate soup is brimming with goodness.

3	large onions, thinly sliced (about 16 ounces [450g])
2	ounces (50g) butter *or* margarine
2	cloves garlic, minced
29	fluid ounces (870ml) tinned beef broth
1	tablespoon Worcestershire sauce
¼	teaspoon pepper
4	½-inch-thick (1cm) slices French bread, toasted and cut into quarters
4	ounces (110g) grated Swiss *or* Gruyère cheese
2	tablespoons grated Parmesan cheese

In a large saucepan combine onions, butter or margarine, and garlic. Cover and cook over low heat, stirring occasionally, for 20 to 25 minutes or till onions are tender (see photo 1).

Stir in beef broth, Worcestershire sauce, and pepper (see photo 2). Bring to boiling; reduce heat (see photo 3). Cover and simmer for 15 minutes.

Ladle soup into 4 ovenproof soup bowls. Top each serving with 4 pieces of toasted bread (see photo 4). Sprinkle each serving with *one-quarter* of the grated Swiss or Gruyère cheese and then *one-quarter* of the Parmesan cheese. Bake in a 500°F (250°C) gas mark 10 oven for 1 to 2 minutes or till cheese is melted. Makes 4 main-dish servings.

1 Cook the onion slices in the butter or margarine until they are tender and yellowish, and their appearance changes from opaque to translucent, as shown. Don't wait for the onion slices to turn brown or they will be overdone.

2 Skip the hours of simmering once necessary for tasty soups by using tinned broth for the soup base. You can substitute homemade broth, or instant bouillon granules or bouillon cubes dissolved in water if you prefer.

3 Using high heat and no lid bring the food to boiling. Boiling is the stage where many bubbles rise vigorously to the surface and break.

Lower the heat until the mixture is simmering. Simmering is the stage where only a few bubbles are formed and they burst below the surface.

4 Arrange the quarters of toasted bread atop the hot soup, overlapping the pieces slightly in the centre of the dish if necessary.

The bread and cheese topping will be easier to eat when the bread has been cut into quarters rather than left in one large piece.

Oriental Chicken-Vegetable Soup

Only a few minutes of chopping plus 4 minutes of simmering and you have a fancy Oriental meal when you're ready to eat.

29 fluid ounces (870ml) tinned chicken broth
1 medium carrot, thinly sliced
2 ounces (50g) thinly sliced or coarsely chopped, peeled daikon *or* radish
1 tablespoon soy sauce
½ teaspoon grated root ginger *or* ⅛ teaspoon ground ginger
5 ounces (150g) cubed cooked chicken
4 ounces (110g) tofu (fresh bean curd), cut into ½-inch (1cm) cubes
2 ounces (50g) torn spinach
3 ounces (75g) sliced fresh mushrooms
2 spring onions, sliced

In a large saucepan combine chicken broth, carrot, daikon or radish, soy sauce, and root ginger or ground ginger (see photo 2, page 26). Bring to boiling; reduce heat (see photo 3, page 27). Cover and simmer for 3 minutes.

Stir in cubed chicken, tofu, spinach, mushrooms, and spring onions. Return mixture to boiling; reduce heat. Cover and simmer 1 minute more or until vegetables are tender. Makes 4 main-dish servings.

Corkscrew Vegetable Soup

29 fluid ounces (870ml) tinned beef broth
4 ounces (110g) sliced carrots
6 fluid ounces (165ml) beer
2½ ounces (60g) sliced celery
4 ounces (110g) chopped onion
2 ounces (50g) corkscrew macaroni
½ teaspoon dried basil, crushed
Dash pepper
1½ ounces (40g) sliced fresh mushrooms

In a large saucepan combine beef broth, carrots, beer, celery, onion, corkscrew macaroni, basil, and pepper (see photo 2, page 26). Bring to boiling; reduce heat (see photo 3, page 27). Cover and simmer for 8 to 10 minutes or until macaroni is almost tender and carrots are crisp-tender (see photo 2, page 15). Stir in mushrooms. Cover and simmer 2 minutes more. Makes 6 servings.

Celery-Spinach Soup

For a favourable first impression, serve this elegant, sophisticated soup.

14½ fluid ounces (400ml) tinned chicken broth
6 ounces (175g) thinly sliced celery
2 ounces (50g) chopped onion
⅛ teaspoon pepper
5 ounces (150g) coarsely chopped spinach
3 fluid ounces (80ml) dry white wine
Grated Parmesan cheese

In a large saucepan combine chicken broth, celery, onion, and pepper (see photo 2, page 26). Bring to boiling; reduce heat (see photo 3, page 27). Cover and simmer about 10 minutes or until vegetables are tender.

Stir in spinach. Cook 2 minutes more. Stir in wine; heat through. Ladle soup into 4 soup bowls. Sprinkle generously with Parmesan cheese. Makes 4 servings.

Jambalaya Soup

Jambalaya is from jambon, the French word for ham. However, a traditional jambalaya also includes prawns, rice and tomatoes.

1	pound (450g) smoked pork hocks *or* meaty ham bones
32	fluid ounces (900ml) water
2	cloves garlic, minced
1	teaspoon dried thyme, crushed
¼	teaspoon ground red pepper
1	bay leaf
½	pound (225g) sliced okra
29	ounces (800g) tinned tomatoes, cut up
8	ounces (225g) chopped celery
4	ounces (110g) chopped onion
2	ounces (50g) long grain rice
2	tablespoons tomato puree
½	pound (225g) frozen cooked prawns

In a large saucepan combine pork hocks or meaty ham bones, water, garlic, thyme, red pepper, and bay leaf. Bring to boiling; reduce heat (see photo 3, page 27). Cover and simmer for 45 minutes.

Remove pork hocks or ham bones. Cool slightly. Cut off meat and chop. Discard bones.

Return meat to the saucepan. Stir in okra, *undrained* tomatoes, celery, onion, *uncooked* rice, and tomato puree. Return to boiling; reduce heat. Cover and simmer about 15 minutes or until vegetables are almost tender.

Add frozen prawns. Cover; simmer for 2 to 3 minutes more or until heated through. Remove bay leaf. Makes 6 main-dish servings.

Corn and Squash Soup

Use any kind of winter squash—acorn, butternut, or Hubbard.

11	fluid ounces (300ml) condensed chicken broth
11	fluid ounces (300ml) water
6	ounces (175g) fresh *or* frozen baby butter beans
4	ounces (110g) chopped onion
⅛	teaspoon pepper
1	pound (450g) cubed, peeled, seeded winter squash
2	medium fresh corn on the cob *or* 9 ounces (250g) frozen sweet corn
	Croutons (optional)

In a large saucepan combine condensed chicken broth, water, butter beans, onion, and pepper (see photo 2, page 26). Bring to boiling; reduce heat (see photo 3, page 27). Cover and simmer for 5 minutes. Add squash. Simmer about 7 minutes more or until beans are almost tender.

Meanwhile, use a sharp knife to cut off just the kernel tips from the fresh corn, then scrape the cob with the dull edge of the knife. Add corn to soup. Return to boiling; reduce heat. Cover and simmer about 3 minutes more or until vegetables are tender. Mash vegetables with a fork to thicken soup. Ladle into soup bowls. Sprinkle with croutons, if desired. Makes 4 to 6 servings.

Under the Heat

You'll do a double take with these classy side-dish vegetables. Quick as a wink, the vegetables will go from grill pan to tabletop.

Being both fast and easy, this cooking method is twice as nice. So next time you're looking for double-delicious vegetables—grill.

Aubergine Pizzas

Aubergine Pizzas

1 **medium aubergine (about 1 pound [450g])**
  Cooking oil
8 **ounces (225g) tinned pizza sauce**
4 **ounces (110g) grated mozzarella cheese**
  Grated Parmesan cheese (optional)

Peel aubergine, if desired. Cut aubergine into ½-inch (1cm) -thick slices (see photo 1). Place slices on the unheated rack of a grill pan. Brush tops lightly with cooking oil (see photo 2).

Place aubergine 4 to 5 inches (10 to 13cm) from the heat (see photo 3). Grill for 6 to 8 minutes or until lightly browned. Turn slices. Brush lightly with oil. Grill for 6 to 8 minutes more or until tender.

Spoon *1 heaped tablespoon* pizza sauce over each aubergine slice (see photo 4). Top slices with mozzarella cheese. Sprinkle with Parmesan cheese, if desired. Broil about 1 minute more or until cheese just starts to melt. Serve warm. Makes 5 or 6 servings.

2 Lightly brush the tops of the aubergine slices with cooking oil before grilling to prevent the aubergine from drying out or shrivelling.

1 Slice the aubergine into even ½-inch (1cm) pieces. If you want, you can peel the vegetable before slicing. However, the peel adds colour and helps hold the slice together when it's cooked.

3 Adjust the grill pan so the aubergine will be between 4 and 5 inches (10 and 13cm) from the heat. Measure from the grill unit to the top surface of the food.

Grilled Tomatoes

Serve crumb-topped tomatoes with meat loaf or fish.

2 **large tomatoes**
¾ **ounce (15g) soft bread crumbs**
3 **tablespoons snipped parsley**
2 **tablespoons grated Parmesan cheese**
¼ **teaspoon dried basil, crushed**
  Dash pepper
1 **tablespoon butter *or* margarine, melted**

Core tomatoes. Peel, if desired. Cut each tomato into ¾-inch (2cm) -thick slices (see photo 1). In a small bowl combine bread crumbs, parsley, Parmesan cheese, basil, and pepper. Stir in melted butter or margarine.

Place tomato slices on the unheated rack of a grill pan. Sprinkle crumb mixture evenly atop tomato slices. Place tomatoes 4 to 5 inches (10 to 13cm) from the heat (see photo 3). Grill for 3 to 4 minutes or until heated through and crumb topping is lightly browned. Serve warm. Makes 4 servings.

4 Carefully spoon the topping onto the vegetable slices, then spread the topping to within ⅛ inch (3mm) of the edge of each slice.

Vegetables From the Bakery

What's satisfying, sweet, *and* special? Fresh-from-the-oven baked goodies with the flavour of favourite vegetables.

Cakes and breads are the perfect place to use succulent vegetables because grated vegetables add flavour, moistness, and a natural sweetness.

Sunshine Carrot Cake

Sunshine Carrot Cake

An easy alternative to icing a cake is to cut out a simple pattern on a sheet of paper. Place the pattern on the cake and sift icing sugar over the top. Carefully remove the pattern to reveal a design of pure sweetness.

½ **pound (225g) carrots (3 to 4 medium)**
7 **ounces (200g) plain flour**
12 **ounces (350g) caster sugar**
1½ **teaspoons baking powder**
¾ **teaspoon ground cinnamon**
½ **teaspoon bicarbonate of soda**
3 **beaten eggs**
4 **fluid ounces (110ml) cooking oil**
2 **tablespoons milk**
¾ **teaspoon finely grated lemon peel**
Cream Cheese Icing (optional)
Pecan halves (optional)
Lemon peel twist (optional)

Grease the bottom and *halfway* up the sides of a 9x9x2-inch (23x23x5cm) baking tin (see photo 1). Lightly flour the tin. Finely grate enough carrot to measure 8 ounces (225g) (see photo 2). Set aside.

In a large mixing bowl stir together flour, sugar, baking powder, cinnamon, and soda. In another bowl beat together eggs, cooking oil, milk, and lemon peel. Stir in grated carrot; mix well. Add the carrot mixture to the flour mixture; mix well (see photo 3).

Pour batter into the prepared tin. Bake in a 325°F (170°C) gas mark 3 oven for 35 to 40 minutes or until a wooden toothpick inserted near the centre comes out clean (see photo 4). Cool 10 minutes on a wire rack. Remove cake from tin; cool thoroughly on a wire rack. Frost with Cream Cheese Icing and garnish with pecan halves and a lemon peel twist, if desired. Makes 9 servings.

Cream Cheese Icing: In a small mixer bowl combine 3 ounces (75g) *cream cheese,* 2 ounces (50g) *butter or margarine,* and 1 teaspoon *vanilla.* Beat until light and fluffy. Gradually add 8 ounces (225g) sifted *icing sugar,* beating until smooth. Spread over cooled cake.

1 Brush lard over the bottom and *halfway* up the sides of the tin. Greasing the tin only halfway up the sides gives cakes and breads smooth, even edges.

2 Rub the carrot across the grater from top to bottom, applying a little pressure on the carrot. Use the smallest holes so you have fine pieces for the cakes and breads.

3 Pour the carrot mixture into the bowl containing the dry ingredients. Then stir with a spoon until the ingredients are well mixed.

Whole Wheat-Courgette Bread

½ **pound (225g) courgette (1 medium)**
5 **ounces (150g) plain flour**
2½ **ounces (75g) whole wheat flour**
1 **teaspoon ground cinnamon**
½ **teaspoon bicarbonate of soda**
¼ **teaspoon baking powder**
¼ **teaspoon salt**
¼ **teaspoon ground ginger**
1 **beaten egg**
8 **ounces (225g) caster sugar**
2 **fluid ounces (55ml) cooking oil**
¾ **teaspoon finely grated lemon peel**
2¾ **ounces (65g) chopped walnuts**

Grease the bottom and *halfway* up the sides of an 8x4x2-inch (20x10x5cm) loaf tin (see photo 1). Finely grate enough unpeeled courgette to measure ½ pound (225g) (see photo 2). Set aside.

In a large mixing bowl stir together plain flour, whole wheat flour, cinnamon, soda, baking powder, salt, and ginger. In another bowl beat together egg, sugar, cooking oil, and lemon peel. Stir in grated courgette. Add courgette mixture to flour mixture; mix well (see photo 3). Stir in walnuts.

Pour batter into the prepared tin. Bake in a 350°F (180°C) gas mark 4 oven for 55 to 60 minutes or until a wooden toothpick inserted near the centre comes out clean (see photo 4). Cool 10 minutes on a wire rack. Remove bread from tin; cool thoroughly on a wire rack. For a softer crust, wrap bread and store at room temperature overnight before slicing. Makes 1 loaf (12 servings).

4 To see if the cake is ready, insert a wooden toothpick near the centre. The cake is done when the toothpick has no batter clinging to it.

Steaming Along

All aboard! You'll know you're on the right track when you sample these tasty steamed vegetables.

The ancient cooking method of steaming is still chugging along today, popular as ever. That's because it's powered by steam, a gentle heat that allows the vegetables to retain their shape and freshness.

Next time you're at a crossing, trying to decide how to prepare your vegetables—steam ahead!

Sweet-Sour Cabbage

Sweet-Sour Cabbage

A surefire accompaniment for grilled bratwurst, knack-wurst, or Polish sausages.

1 **medium head cabbage (about 2 pounds [900g])**

1 **large sweet red pepper *or* green pepper (8 ounces [225g]), cut into ¾-inch (2cm) pieces**

⅓ **ounce (35g) packed soft brown sugar**

1 **tablespoon cornflour**

2 **fluid ounces (55ml) chicken broth**

2 **fluid ounces (55ml) red wine vinegar**

1 **tablespoon water**

2 **teaspoons soy sauce**

½ **teaspoon grated root ginger *or* ⅛ teaspoon ground ginger**

1 **clove garlic, minced**

1 Add water to the pan until the water level is just below, but doesn't touch, the steamer basket. With the steaming technique, the vegetables are never in the boiling water.

2 Once the water is boiling, lower the vegetables into the steamer basket with tongs or a large spoon.

Place steamer basket in a covered casserole; add water to just below basket (see photo 1). Bring water to boiling. Cut cabbage into 8 wedges; remove core. Place cabbage wedges in steamer basket (see photo 2). Cover and steam for 5 minutes. Add red or green pepper (see photo 3). Cover and steam for 5 to 8 minutes more or until vegetables are crisp-tender.

Meanwhile, in a small saucepan combine soft brown sugar and cornflour. Stir in chicken broth, vinegar, water, soy sauce, root ginger or ground ginger, and garlic. Cook and stir until thickened and bubbly, then cook and stir 2 minutes more (see photo 4).

Carefully remove steamer basket from casserole (see photo 5). Transfer vegetables to dinner plates or a warm serving dish. Spoon sauce over vegetables. Makes 4 servings.

3 Steam the cabbage wedges for a few minutes before adding the red or green pepper. Adding the vegetables in stages ensures that they will all be tender at the same time.

4 When the sauce becomes thick and bubbly, continue to cook and stir a few minutes longer. This fully cooks the sauce so it doesn't taste starchy.

5 Grasp the stem of the steamer basket and lift the vegetables out of the pan. Wearing an oven glove helps protect your arm and hand from the steam.

Asparagus with Almond Sauce

1	pound (450g) asparagus
1	tablespoon butter *or* margarine
1	ounce (10g) slivered almonds
1	teaspoon cornflour
3	fluid ounces (80ml) water
2	teaspoons lemon juice
½	teaspoon instant chicken bouillon granules
	Dash pepper

Place steamer basket in a large saucepan; add water to just below basket (*see* photo 1, page 40). Bring water to boiling.

Wash fresh asparagus and scrape off scales, if desired. Break off woody bases at point where spears snap easily; discard bases. Place asparagus in steamer basket (*see* photo 2, page 40). Cover and steam for 8 to 10 minutes or until crisp-tender.

Meanwhile, make sauce. In a small saucepan melt butter or margarine. Add almonds. Cook over medium heat, stirring constantly, for 3 to 5 minutes or until golden. Stir in cornflour. Add water, lemon juice, bouillon granules, and pepper. Cook and stir until thickened and bubbly, then cook and stir 2 minutes more (*see* photo 4, page 41).

Carefully remove steamer basket from pan (*see* photo 5, page 41). Transfer asparagus to a warm serving dish. Spoon sauce over asparagus. Makes 4 servings.

Cheesy Chokes And Leeks

Discover the nutty flavour of Jerusalem artichokes.

1	pound (450g) Jerusalem artichokes
5	ounces (150g) thinly sliced leeks
6	fluid ounces (165ml) milk
2	teaspoons cornflour
⅛	teaspoon salt
	Dash white pepper
2	ounces (50g) grated Swiss *or* Gruyère cheeses
2	ounces (50g) pimento, drained and chopped

Place steamer basket in a large saucepan; add water to just below basket (*see* photo 1, page 40). Bring water to boiling.

Thoroughly scrub Jerusalem artichokes (*see* photo 1, page 21). Cut into ¼-inch-thick (.5cm) slices. Place Jerusalem artichokes and leeks in steamer basket (*see* photo 2, page 40). Cover and steam for 8 to 10 minutes or until vegetables are crisp-tender.

Meanwhile, make sauce. In a small saucepan combine milk, cornflour, salt, and pepper. Cook and stir until thickened and bubbly, then cook and stir 2 minutes more (*see* photo 4, page 41). Add Swiss or Gruyère cheese and pimento; stir over low heat until cheese is melted.

Carefully remove steamer basket from pan (*see* photo 5, page 41). Transfer vegetables to a warm serving dish. Pour cheese sauce over vegetables; toss gently to coat. Makes 6 servings.

◄ *Asparagus with Almond Sauce*

Broccoli with Brie Sauce

Tastes like fondue on broccoli or cauliflower.

1   **pound (450g) broccoli *or* cauliflower florets (see photo 1, page 8)**
1   **tablespoon butter *or* margarine**
1   **tablespoon plain flour**
⅛   **teaspoon salt**
    Dash white pepper
4   **fluid ounces (110ml) milk**
2   **ounces (50g) Brie cheese (rind trimmed), cubed**
1   **tablespoon dry white wine**

Place steamer basket in a large saucepan; add water to just below basket (see photo 1, page 40). Bring water to boiling.

Place broccoli or cauliflower florets in steamer basket (see photo 2, page 40). Cover and steam 10 to 12 minutes for broccoli or 8 to 10 minutes for cauliflower or until crisp-tender.

To make sauce, in a small saucepan melt butter or margarine. Stir in flour, salt, and pepper. Add milk all at once. Cook and stir until thickened and bubbly; cook and stir 1 minute more (see photo 4, page 41). Add Brie cheese; stir over low heat until melted. Stir in wine.

Carefully remove steamer basket from pan (see photo 5, page 41). Transfer broccoli or cauliflower to a warm serving bowl. Pour Brie sauce over vegetable. Makes 5 or 6 servings.

Creamed Parsnips And Peas

Imagine a slightly sweet, pale carrot and what have you got? A parsnip.

12   **ounces (350g) parsnips**
10   **ounces (275g) frozen peas**
2   **ounces (50g) chopped onion**
2   **tablespoons butter *or* margarine**
1   **ounce (25g) plain flour**
⅛   **teaspoon salt**
⅛   **teaspoon white pepper**
8   **fluid ounces (220ml) milk**

Place steamer basket in a large saucepan; add water to just below basket (see photo 1, page 40). Bring water to boiling.

Wash, trim ends, and scrape or peel parsnips. Cut parsnips into ¼-inch (.5cm) slices. Place parsnips and frozen peas in steamer basket (see photo 2, page 40). Cover and steam about 12 minutes or until vegetables are crisp-tender.

Meanwhile, make sauce. In a small saucepan cook onion in hot butter or margarine until tender but not brown. Stir in flour, salt, and pepper. Add milk all at once. Cook and stir until thickened and bubbly, then cook and stir 1 minute more (see photo 4, page 41).

Carefully remove steamer basket from pan (see photo 5, page 41). Transfer vegetables to a warm serving dish. Pour cream sauce over vegetables; stir gently to coat. Makes 6 servings.

New Potatoes with Mustard Sauce

Select your favourite mustard to flavour the sauce.

1 pound (450g) whole tiny new potatoes
      (about 10 potatoes)
2 tablespoons finely chopped onion
2 tablespoons butter *or* margarine
1 tablespoon plain flour
¼ teaspoon salt
      Dash pepper
8 fluid ounces (220ml) milk
1 tablespoon French mustard *or*
      prepared mustard
1 teaspoon horseradish sauce

Place steamer basket in a large saucepan; add water to just below basket (see photo 1, page 40). Bring water to boiling.

Scrub potatoes (see photo 1, page 21). Cut any large potatoes in half. Remove a narrow strip of peel around centre of each potato. Place potatoes in steamer basket (see photo 2, page 40). Cover and steam for 20 to 25 minutes or until potatoes are tender.

Meanwhile, make sauce. In a small saucepan cook onion in hot butter or margarine until tender but not brown. Stir in flour, salt, and pepper. Add milk all at once. Cook and stir until thickened and bubbly, then cook and stir 1 minute more (see photo 4, page 41). Stir in mustard and horseradish sauce.

Carefully remove steamer basket from pan (see photo 5, page 41). Transfer potatoes to a warm serving dish. Pour mustard sauce over potatoes. Makes 4 servings.

Lemon-Basil Carrots

Here's a jewel of a sauce—so simple yet so versatile. Just vary the herb and use it on other vegetables. For starters, try thyme with broccoli, tarragon with parsnips, and garlic with beans.

6 to 8 carrots
2 tablespoons butter *or* margarine
1 tablespoon lemon juice
¾ teaspoon snipped fresh basil *or*
      ¼ teaspoon dried basil, crushed

Place steamer basket in a large saucepan; add water to just below basket (see photo 1, page 40). Bring water to boiling.

Wash, trim ends, and peel or scrub carrots. Thinly slice enough carrots to make 12 ounces (350g) (see photo 2, page 8). Place carrots in steamer basket (see photo 2, page 40). Cover and steam about 15 minutes or until carrots are crisp-tender.

Meanwhile, make sauce. In a small saucepan melt butter or margarine. Stir in lemon juice and fresh or dried basil.

Carefully remove steamer basket from pan (see photo 5, page 41). Transfer carrots to a warm serving bowl. Pour sauce over carrots; stir gently to coat. Makes 4 servings.

Stuffed Specialities

With an all-star line-up of squash, peppers, aubergines, and turnips, your dinner-time fans will cheer.

Everyone is a winner when you pack a savoury filling into one of these vegetables. Putting it all together into one scrumptious package gives these dishes a double advantage.

If you have trouble finding some of these vegetables in your local supermarket, try growing them in your vegetable garden. It'll be worth the trouble—from the first to the last mouthful.

Curried Sausage-Meat-Stuffed Squash

Curried Sausage-Meat-Stuffed Squash

2	medium acorn squash (about 1½ pounds [700g] each)
10	fluid ounces (275ml) water
4	ounces (110g) regular brown rice
1	ounce (25g) raisins
1	teaspoon instant chicken bouillon granules
1	pound (450g) bulk sausage meat
1	small onion, chopped
2	ounces (50g) chutney
1	teaspoon curry powder
1⅓	ounces (30g) coarsely chopped peanuts
	Celery leaves (optional)
	Apple wedges (optional)

Cut squash in half lengthwise. Remove seeds from squash (see photo 1). Place squash, cut side down, in a large baking tin. Bake in a 350°F (180°C) gas mark 4 oven about 50 minutes or until tender.

Meanwhile, in a small saucepan combine water, brown rice, raisins, and chicken bouillon granules. Bring to the boil, then cover and reduce heat. Simmer for 40 to 50 minutes or until rice is tender and water is absorbed.

In a large frying pan cook sausage meat and chopped onion until meat is brown and onion is tender. Drain off fat (see photo 2). Return sausage meat mixture to the frying pan. Stir in chutney and curry powder. Cook and stir over medium heat for 2 minutes. Stir in cooked rice and peanuts.

Scoop out pulp from squash halves, if necessary, to make ½-inch (1cm) -thick shells (see photo 3). (Reserve pulp to use as a vegetable side dish another time.) Spoon sausage-meat mixture into squash shells (see photo 4). Bake squash, covered, for 20 to 25 minutes more.

Transfer squash to dinner plates. Garnish each with celery leaves and apple wedges, if desired. Pass *sliced spring onions* and chopped peanuts to sprinkle atop stuffed squash, if desired. Makes 4 main-dish servings.

1 Using a sturdy tablespoon, scoop out the seeds and scrape out the strings from the cavity of each acorn squash half, as shown. Discard the seeds and strings.

2 To drain fat off the browned meat, set a colander over a grease can or disposable container. Transfer the meat mixture from the frying pan into the colander and allow a few minutes to drain.

3 Scrape out just enough of the squash pulp to leave a ½-inch-thick (1cm) shell, as shown. The filling is generous so some of the pulp must be removed to make room for all of the filling.

4 Return the squash shells to the baking tin, then lightly spoon the sausage-meat filling into the cavity of each shell, piling the filling high, if necessary.

German-Style Stuffed Turnips

6   turnips (10 to 13 ounces [275 to 375g] each)
2   tablespoons butter *or* margarine
1   tablespoon plain flour
⅛   teaspoon salt
     Dash pepper
4   fluid ounces (110ml) milk
1   ounce (25g) grated Swiss cheese
8   ounces (225g) sauerkraut, rinsed, drained, and snipped
¼   teaspoon caraway seed
     Melted butter *or* margarine
2⅔ ounces (70g) crushed crispy rye crackers
1   tablespoon snipped parsley

In a covered casserole bring 24 fluid ounces (720ml) lightly salted water to boiling. Peel turnips; add to casserole. Return to boiling; reduce heat. Simmer, covered, about 25 minutes or until tender. Drain turnips. Scoop out pulp from turnip centres, leaving ¼- to ½-inch (½-to 1cm) shells (see photo 3, page 49). Finely chop enough turnip pulp to measure 4 ounces (110g); set aside. (Reserve remaining turnip pulp to use as a vegetable side dish another time.)

In a small saucepan melt *1 tablespoon* butter or margarine. Stir in flour, salt, and pepper. Add milk all at once. Cook and stir until thickened and bubbly; cook and stir 1 minute more. Add cheese; stir over low heat until melted. Stir in turnip pulp, sauerkraut, and caraway.

Place turnip shells in a greased 12x7½x2-inch (30x19x5cm) baking tin. Spoon filling into turnip shells (see photo 4, page 49). Brush with melted butter or margarine. Bake, covered, in a 350°F (180°C) gas mark 4 oven for 15 to 20 minutes or until heated through.

Meanwhile, in a small saucepan melt remaining 1 tablespoon butter or margarine; stir in crushed crackers and parsley. Sprinkle cracker mixture atop turnips. Bake, uncovered, 5 minutes more. Makes 6 servings.

Orzo- and Feta-Stuffed Pepper Shells

Shop for orzo, also called rosamarina, in the pasta section of your supermarket. Look for a tiny pasta that resembles grains of rice.

3   ounces (75g) orzo *or* small shell macaroni
2   large green peppers
1   tablespoon butter *or* margarine
1   clove garlic, minced
1   tablespoon plain flour
4   fluid ounces (110ml) milk
2   ounces (50g) crumbled feta *or* blue cheese
4   ounces (110g) fresh tomato, seeded and chopped (1 small)
3   tablespoons snipped parsley
2   tablespoons sliced spring onion
½   teaspoon dried basil, crushed
¼   teaspoon salt
     Dash pepper

Cook orzo or small shell macaroni in boiling lightly salted water, allowing 5 to 8 minutes for orzo or 8 to 9 minutes for macaroni. Drain well.

Meanwhile, cut green peppers in half lengthwise. Remove stems, seeds, and membranes (see photo 1, page 48). In a large saucepan cook green peppers, covered, in a large amount of boiling water for 3 minutes. Drain peppers; invert on kitchen papers.

For filling, in a small saucepan melt butter or margarine. Add garlic and cook 1 minute; stir in flour. Add milk all at once. Cook and stir until thickened and bubbly. Stir in feta or blue cheese; remove from heat. Stir in orzo or macaroni, tomato, parsley, onion, basil, salt, and pepper.

Place green pepper shells in an 8x8x2-inch (20x20x5cm) baking dish. Spoon filling into shells (see photo 4, page 49). Bake, covered, in a 350°F (180°C) gas mark 4 oven for 20 to 25 minutes or until heated through. Serves 4.

Crab- and Avocado- Stuffed Courgette

Impressing your friends with an elegant luncheon is easy when you serve this make-ahead entrée.

6 ounces (175g) frozen or tinned crab-meat *or* salad-style crab-flavoured fish
3 medium courgettes (about 6 ounces [175g] each)
1 small avocado, halved, seeded, and peeled
¼ teaspoon finely grated lemon peel
1 tablespoon lemon juice
2 ounces (50g) thinly sliced celery
1 tablespoon thinly sliced spring onion
3 tablespoons mayonnaise *or* salad dressing
¼ teaspoon onion salt
¼ teaspoon dried dill
   Dash pepper

Thaw frozen crabmeat or crab-flavoured fish; drain well. (Or drain tinned crabmeat.) Cut courgettes in half lengthwise. With a paring knife make a cut around each courgette half about ¼ inch (.5cm) from the outside edge. Then scoop out pulp, leaving a ¼-inch (.5cm) shell (*see* photo 3, page 49). Chop enough pulp to measure 4 ounces (110g); set aside. (Reserve remaining pulp to use as a vegetable side dish another time.)

Place halved courgettes, cut side down, in a 12-inch (30cm) frying pan. Add 4 fluid ounces (110ml) water. Cover and simmer for 3 to 5 minutes or until courgettes are tender. Drain courgettes; cover and chill thoroughly.

Meanwhile, cut crabmeat or fish into bite-size pieces. Cube avocado. In a medium bowl combine avocado, lemon peel, and lemon juice; toss gently. Add chopped courgettes, crabmeat or fish, celery, and spring onion; toss to combine. In a small bowl stir mayonnaise or salad dressing, onion salt, dill, and pepper. Add to avocado-crab mixture. Stir gently.

To serve, stir crab filling. Spoon filling into courgette shells, mounding as necessary (*see* photo 4, page 49). Makes 3 main-dish servings.

Savoury Stuffed Aubergine

2 medium aubergines (about 1 pound [450g] each)
12 ounces (350g) minced lamb *or* beef
4 ounces (110g) chopped onion (1 medium)
1 clove garlic, minced
7½ ounces (210g) tinned tomatoes, cut up
1 large carrot, grated
4 ounces (110g) chopped green pepper
3 ounces (75g) quick-method couscous
1 ounce (25g) snipped parsley
2 tablespoons water
1 teaspoon dried oregano, crushed
¾ teaspoon salt
¼ teaspoon pepper
2 ounces (50g) grated mozzarella cheese
1½ ounces (40g) grated Parmesan cheese
2 well-beaten eggs

Cut aubergines in half lengthwise. Scoop out pulp, leaving ½-inch (1cm) shells (*see* photo 3, page 49). Chop pulp; set aside. Place shells, cut side down, in a 12-inch (30cm) frying pan; add water to pan to a depth of 1 inch (2.5cm). Bring to boiling. Simmer, covered, for 3 to 5 minutes or until just tender. Drain shells; set aside.

In the same frying pan cook lamb or beef, onion, and garlic until meat is brown and onion is tender. Drain off fat (*see* photo 2, page 48). Return meat mixture to frying pan. Add chopped aubergines, *undrained* tomatoes, carrot, green pepper, *uncooked* couscous, parsley, water, oregano, salt, and pepper. Bring to boiling; reduce heat. Simmer, covered, for 10 minutes. Remove from heat. Stir in mozzarella cheese, *half* of the Parmesan cheese, and eggs.

Place aubergine shells in a 13x9x2-inch (32.5x23x5cm) baking tin. Spoon meat mixture into shells (*see* photo 4, page 49). Bake, covered, in a 350°F (180°C) gas mark 4 oven for 20 minutes. Sprinkle with remaining Parmesan cheese. Bake 5 minutes more. Makes 4 main-dish servings.

Microwave Magic

Abracadabra! With a push of a button and a wave of a wooden spoon, you and your ardent assistant can make vegetable dishes appear before your very eyes. Your assistant? The microwave oven, of course.

The microwave's speed and efficiency trim cooking times without wasting energy. So, when you're ready to add magic to mealtime, call on your microwave oven.

Spaghetti Squash with Tomato-Dill Sauce

Spaghetti Squash with Tomato-Dill Sauce

Great news for waist watchers—spaghetti squash (also known as vegetable spaghetti) makes a delicious, low-calorie alternative to pasta!

1	medium spaghetti squash (about 3 pounds [1kg350g])
2	tablespoons water
2	ounces (50g) chopped onion
1	tablespoon butter *or* margarine
1½	teaspoons snipped fresh dill *or* ½ teaspoon dried dill
1	tablespoon cornflour
7½	ounces (210g) tinned tomatoes, cut up
3	tablespoons chilli sauce
	Parsley sprigs (optional)

Cut spaghetti squash in half lengthwise. (Reserve 1 squash half for another use.*)

Remove seeds from remaining squash half (see photo 1, page 48). Place squash, cut side down, in a microwave-safe baking dish.

Add water (see photo 1). Cover (see photo 2). Micro-cook on 100% power (HIGH) for 10 to 14 minutes or until pulp can just be pierced with a fork, giving dish a half-turn twice (see photo 3). Let stand 10 minutes.

Meanwhile, make sauce. In a small microwave-safe bowl combine onion, butter or margarine, and dill. Cook, uncovered, on high for 2 minutes. Stir in cornflour. Stir in *undrained* tomatoes and chilli sauce. Cook, uncovered, on high for 2 to 3 minutes or until thickened and bubbly, stirring after every minute.

Use a fork to separate squash pulp into strands (see photo 4). Arrange squash in a ring shape on a serving dish. Spoon sauce atop squash. Place the parsley sprigs in centre of ring, if desired. Makes 4 servings.

***Note:** Place reserved squash half in an airtight container or polythene bag; seal. Store in the refrigerator for up to 3 days. Micro-cook according to the directions above and serve as a buttered side-dish vegetable or with warm spaghetti sauce.

1 Adding water to vegetables creates steam during the micro-cooking. The steam helps the vegetable cook faster and more evenly.

2 Substitute a covering of microwave-safe clear clingfilm when a dish does not have a lid. Create a small vent for steam to escape through by folding back one of the corners of the clingfilm.

3 When it is not possible to stir a food, just turn the dish around. This gives the food a different pattern of microwaves to help it cook more evenly.

4 Twist the fork slightly and the pulp of the cooked spaghetti squash will easily separate into spaghetti-like strands. Then rake the squash strands out of the shell.

Wilted Spinach Salad

Wilt the spinach just before serving the meal so you can eat the salad immediately at its peak of flavour.

3 rashers streaky bacon
2⅔ fluid ounces (70ml) milk
1 tablespoon plain flour
1 tablespoon prepared mustard
2 teaspoons caster sugar
   Dash pepper
2 tablespoons vinegar
24 ounces (450 to 560g) torn spinach
3 ounces (75g) sliced fresh mushrooms
2 tablespoons water

Place 2 microwave-safe kitchen papers in a shallow microwave-safe baking dish. Arrange streaky bacon atop kitchen papers; cover with another kitchen paper. Micro-cook on 100% power (HIGH) for 2½ to 3 minutes. Let stand a few minutes to crisp. Crumble and set aside.

For dressing, in an 8-fluid-ounce (220ml) glass measuring jug stir together milk, flour, mustard, sugar, and pepper. Cook, uncovered, on high about 1½ minutes or until mixture is thickened and bubbly, stirring every 30 seconds. Stir in vinegar; set aside.

Place torn spinach and mushrooms in a large microwave-safe casserole. Add water (see photo 1, page 54). Cook, covered, on high for 1½ to 2 minutes or just until spinach begins to wilt, stirring once. Drain well.

Transfer spinach mixture to a salad bowl. Pour mustard dressing over spinach; toss to coat. Sprinkle with crumbled streaky bacon. Serve immediately. Makes 4 servings.

Harvard Beetroots

Can't beat these sweet beetroots!

4 medium beetroots (about 1¼ pounds [560g])
2 tablespoons water
2 tablespoons vinegar
1 tablespoon caster sugar
1 tablespoon butter *or* margarine
1 teaspoon cornflour
⅛ teaspoon salt

Wash beetroots thoroughly. Peel with a potato peeler; cut into ¼-inch (.5cm) -thick slices or cubes. Place beetroots in a medium microwave-safe casserole. Add water (see photo 1, page 54). Micro-cook, covered, on 100% power (HIGH) for 10 to 12 minutes, stirring once. Drain, reserving liquid. Set beetroots aside.

Add enough water to reserved cooking liquid to measure 2 fluid ounces (55ml). Return liquid to casserole. Stir in vinegar, sugar, butter or margarine, cornflour, and salt. Cook, uncovered, on high for 3 to 4 minutes or until thickened and bubbly, stirring every minute until slightly thickened, then every 30 seconds. Stir in beetroots. Cook, uncovered, on high for 30 to 60 seconds more or until beetroots are heated through. Makes 4 servings.

Mange Tout and Summer Squash

6 **ounces (175g) fresh or frozen mange tout**
6 **ounces (175g) sliced yellow crookneck squash (see photo 2, page 8) *or* courgette**
2 **tablespoons chopped pimento *or* chopped sweet red pepper**
2 **tablespoons water**
3 **tablespoons clear Italian salad dressing**

Wash fresh mange tout. Make a cut across stem ends and pull off strings. Slice fresh or frozen mange tout in half crosswise. Place mange tout, squash or courgette, and pimento or red pepper in a small microwave-safe casserole. Add water (see photo 1, page 54). Micro-cook, covered, on 100% power (HIGH) for 3 to 5 minutes or until crisp-tender, stirring twice. Drain well.

Return vegetables to casserole; stir in Italian salad dressing. Cook, uncovered, on high about 1 minute more or until heated through. Serves 4.

Honeyed Turnips And Apples

Honey and spice and everything nice—that's what tasty recipes are made of.

¾ **pound (350g) turnips, peeled and cut into ½-inch (1cm) cubes**
2 **tablespoons water**
2 **small apples, cored and cut into thin wedges**
2 **tablespoons honey**
2 **tablespoons butter *or* margarine**
⅛ **teaspoon ground cinnamon**
   Dash salt

Place turnips in a medium microwave-safe casserole. Add water (see photo 1, page 54). Micro-cook, covered, on 100% power (HIGH) for 12 to 15 minutes or until tender, stirring once. Drain well in a colander (see photo 3, page 15).

In the same casserole combine apples, honey, butter or margarine, cinnamon, and salt. Cook, covered, on high for 1 to 2 minutes or until apples are just tender, stirring once. Add turnips. Cook on high 1 minute more or until heated through. Stir before serving. Serves 4.

Creole-Style Vegetables

Some like it hot, some not—you decide how much red pepper you like.

4 **ounces (110g) chopped onion**
2 **tablespoons water**
½ **pound (225g) sliced okra**
1½ **ounces (40g) finely chopped celery**
2 **ounces (50g) finely chopped sweet red *or* green pepper**
2 **cloves garlic, minced**
7½ **ounces (210g) tinned tomatoes, cut up**
1 **teaspoon Worcestershire sauce**
⅛ **to ¼ teaspoon ground red pepper**

Place chopped onion in a medium microwave-safe casserole. Add water (see photo 1, page 54). Micro-cook, covered, on 100% power (HIGH) for 1 minute. Add okra, celery, red or green pepper, and garlic. Cook, covered, on high for 5 to 6 minutes or until okra is almost tender, stirring once.

Stir in *undrained* tomatoes, Worcestershire sauce, and ground red pepper. Mix well. Cook, covered, on high for 1½ to 2½ minutes more or until heated through, stirring once. Serves 4.

Sweet Corn Relish

Duplicate the restaurants' relish trays with your own arrangement of sweet corn relish, pickles, cold beetroots, pickled herring, and raw vegetable sticks.

3   **medium fresh corn on the cob *or* 10 ounces (275g) frozen sweet corn**
2   **tablespoons water**
1   **small onion, finely chopped**
2   **tablespoons finely chopped celery**
2   **tablespoons finely chopped green pepper**
2   **tablespoons chopped pimento**
¾   **teaspoon ground turmeric**
½   **teaspoon mustard powder**
2⅔ **ounces (70g) caster sugar**
2⅔ **fluid ounces (65ml) vinegar**
2   **fluid ounces (55ml) water**
2   **teaspoons cornflour**
¼   **teaspoon salt**

With a sharp knife cut off kernel tips from the fresh corn. Place fresh or frozen sweet corn in a medium microwave-safe casserole. Add 2 tablespoons water (see photo 1, page 54). Micro-cook, covered, on 100% power (HIGH) for 6 to 8 minutes or until corn is tender, stirring once. *Do not drain.* Add onion, celery, green pepper, pimento, turmeric, and mustard powder.

In a small bowl stir together sugar, vinegar, 2 fluid ounces (55ml) water, cornflour, and salt. Stir into corn mixture. Cook, uncovered, on high for 6 to 8 minutes or until thickened and bubbly, stirring every minute until slightly thickened, then *every* 30 seconds. Cover; chill at least 4 hours. Makes about 24 ounces (700g) of relish (12 servings).

Note: For longer storage, place in a freezer container, seal, label, and freeze up to 6 months. To use, thaw in the refrigerator.

Artichokes with Citrus Butter

Start off a dinner for two with this classy appetiser.

2   **medium artichokes (about 8 ounces [225g] each)**
    Lemon juice
2   **tablespoons water**
2   **ounces (50g) butter *or* margarine**
¼   **teaspoon finely grated orange peel**
2   **tablespoons orange juice**
1   **tablespoon lemon juice**
    Orange slices (optional)

Wash artichokes, trim stems, and remove loose outer leaves. Cut off 1 inch (2.5cm) of tops. Snip off sharp leaf tips. Brush cut edges of leaves with lemon juice.

Place artichokes in a medium microwave-safe casserole. Add water (see photo 1, page 54). Micro-cook, covered, on 100% power (HIGH) for 6 to 9 minutes or until a leaf pulls out easily, giving dish a half-turn once (see photo 3, page 55). Remove artichokes from the casserole; invert to drain.

Place butter or margarine in a small microwave-safe bowl. Cook, uncovered, on high for 30 to 60 seconds or until melted. Stir in orange peel, orange juice, and 1 tablespoon lemon juice.

Arrange artichokes on salad plates; garnish with orange slices, if desired. Pour butter mixture into 2 small serving bowls or cups. To eat, pull off one leaf at a time and dunk into warm butter. Then, discard the fuzzy choke and eat the artichoke heart (see tip, page 17). Serves 2.

▶   *Artichokes with Citrus Butter*

Simply Smashing Vegetables

Looking for *simply smashing* vegetables? Then have a look here, mate.

Mashing makes the vegetables oh-so-creamy in texture. Any of these recipes creates the perfect match with baked ham, crispy fried fish, grilled steak, or with any favourite meat.

It's a sure bet your family will enjoy these outstanding dishes.

Southern Sweet Potatoes

Southern Sweet Potatoes

4 large sweet potatoes (6 to 8 ounces [175 to 225g] each)
2 tablespoons butter *or* margarine
2 tablespoons orange juice *or* milk
1 tablespoon honey
1 ounce (25g) finely chopped pecans

Scrub potatoes; prick with a fork. Bake in a 425°F (220°C) gas mark 7 oven for 40 to 60 minutes or until done. (*Or*, bake in a 350°F [180°C] gas mark 4 oven for 60 to 70 minutes.)

Cut a slice from the top of each potato; discard peel from slices. Scoop out each potato, leaving a thin shell (see photo 1). Mash potatoes (see photo 2). Add butter, orange juice, honey, and ¼ teaspoon *salt;* continue mashing until very smooth. If piping potatoes, cool slightly.

Place the potato shells in a 10x6x2-inch (25.5x15x5cm) baking dish. Using a decorating bag with a large star tip, pipe mashed potatoes into shells (see photo 3). (*Or*, spoon mashed potatoes into shells.) Sprinkle with nuts. Bake in a 425°F (220°C) gas mark 7 oven for 10 to 15 minutes or until heated through. (*Or*, bake in a 350°F [180°C] gas mark 4 oven for 15 to 20 minutes). Makes 4 servings.

2 Potato Masher: Break up potato pulp with a potato masher, as shown. Add butter, liquid, and seasonings. Then, continue mashing until potatoes are fairly smooth.

Food Mill: Work potato pulp through a food mill or potato ricer. Add butter, liquid, and seasonings. Stir with spoon until fairly smooth.

Electric Mixer: In a mixer bowl beat potato pulp with an electric mixer on low speed until almost smooth. Add butter, liquid, and seasonings. Continue beating until light and fluffy.

1 Use a spoon to scoop out sweet potato pulp leaving only a thin (about ¼-inch [.5cm]) shell. Scrape gently to avoid tearing the shell.

3 To pipe the potatoes, fit a tip onto the decorating bag and fill the bag with the cooled mashed potatoes. Fold the end of the bag to close. Holding the full end of the bag in the palm of your writing hand, press gently to force the potatoes through the tip. Use your other hand to guide the tip.

Curried Cauliflower Puree

A hint of curry and a head of cauliflower are all you need for a sensational vegetable dish.

1   small head cauliflower (about 1 pound [450g])
⅛   teaspoon curry powder

Wash and trim cauliflower. Cut into small florets. In a medium saucepan bring a small amount of lightly salted water to boiling. Add cauliflower. Return to boiling; reduce heat. Cook, covered, for 10 to 12 minutes or until very tender. Drain well in a colander (see photo 3, page 15).

Mash cauliflower using a potato masher or food mill until smooth* (see photo 2, page 62). Return cauliflower to the saucepan; stir in curry powder. Place over low heat; stir constantly until heated through. Spoon caulifower into a serving bowl. Makes 6 servings.

*Note: If desired, place cauliflower in food processor bowl or blender container. Cover; process or blend until smooth, stopping and scraping sides of bowl as necessary. Return cauliflower to saucepan; stir in curry powder. Place over low heat; stir constantly until heated through.

Whipped Turnips

1   pound (450g) turnips
4   ounces (110g) soured cream
2   tablespoons butter *or* margarine
¼   teaspoon salt
⅛   teaspoon ground nutmeg
1   to 2 tablespoons milk
2   tablespoons snipped parsley

Peel and cube turnips. In a medium saucepan bring 1 to 2 inches (2.5 to 5cm) of lightly salted water to boiling. Add turnips. Return to boiling; reduce heat. Cook, covered, about 30 minutes or until tender. Drain well in a colander (see photo 3, page 15).

Mash turnips (see photo 2, page 62). Add soured cream, butter or margarine, salt, and nutmeg. Continue mashing until smooth, adding enough milk to moisten.

Return turnip mixture to saucepan. Place over low heat; stir constantly until heated through. Spoon turnip mixture into a serving bowl. Sprinkle with snipped parsley and additional ground nutmeg, if desired. Makes 4 servings.

Mexican Potatoes

Balance this flavour-packed side dish with a simple entrée, such as grilled or baked chicken or ham.

3   medium potatoes (about 1 pound [450g])
2   ounces (50g) soured cream
2   fluid ounces (55ml) milk
½   teaspoon chilli powder
¼   teaspoon salt
Few dashes bottled hot pepper sauce
1½   ounces (40g) canned diced green chilli peppers, rinsed and drained

Peel and quarter potatoes. In a medium saucepan bring 1 to 2 inches (2.5 to 5cm) of lightly salted water to boiling. Add potatoes. Return to boiling; reduce heat. Cook, covered, 20 to 25 minutes or until tender. Drain.

Mash potatoes (see photo 2, page 62). Add soured cream, milk, chilli powder, salt, and hot pepper sauce. Continue mashing until mixture is smooth. Return mixture to the saucepan; add chilli peppers. Place over low heat; stir constantly until heated through. Spoon into a serving dish. Makes 4 servings.

Mashed Potatoes

A little whipping cream makes every-day mashed potatoes taste extra special.

3 medium potatoes (about 1 pound [450g])
2 tablespoons whipping cream *or* milk
1 tablespoon butter *or* margarine
⅛ teaspoon salt
    Dash pepper

Peel and quarter potatoes. In a medium saucepan bring 1 to 2 inches (2.5 to 5cm) of lightly salted water to boiling. Add potatoes. Return to boiling; reduce heat. Cook, covered, 20 to 25 minutes or until tender. Drain.

Mash potatoes (see photo 2, page 62). Add whipping cream or milk, butter or margarine, salt, and pepper. Continue mashing until smooth. Return potato mixture to saucepan. Place over low heat; stir constantly until heated through. Spoon into a serving dish. Makes 4 servings.

Volcano Potatoes: Prepare Mashed Potatoes as above, *except* double the recipe. Mound potatoes into a greased 8x1½-inch (20x4cm) round baking dish. Make a shallow crater (about 3 inches [7.5cm] wide) in the centre of potatoes. Whip 2 fluid ounces (55ml) *whipping cream* until soft peaks form. Fold 3 ounces (75g) grated *processed or cheddar cheese* into cream. Spoon into the crater. Bake in a 350°F (180°C) gas mark 4 oven about 20 minutes or until browned. Makes 8 servings.

Oriental Turnips

Water chestnuts give just the right crunch.

1 pound (450g) turnips
2 tablespoons butter *or* margarine
1 teaspoon soy sauce
4 ounces (110g) tinned sliced water chestnuts, drained
    Thinly sliced spring onions (optional)

Peel and slice turnips. In a medium saucepan bring 1 to 2 inches (2.5 to 5cm) of lightly salted water to boiling. Add turnips. Return to boiling; reduce heat. Cook, covered, 20 to 25 minutes or until turnips are tender. Drain well in a colander (see photo 3, page 15).

Mash turnips* (see photo 2, page 62). Add butter or margarine and soy sauce. Continue mashing until turnips are smooth.

Return turnip mixture to saucepan; add water chestnuts. Place over low heat; stir constantly until heated through and most of the liquid is evaporated. Spoon into a serving bowl. Sprinkle with spring onions, if desired. Makes 4 servings.

*****Note:** If desired, place turnips in a food processor bowl or blender container. Add butter or margarine and soy sauce. Cover; process or blend until smooth, stopping and scraping sides of bowl as necessary. Return turnip mixture to saucepan; add water chestnuts. Heat as directed above.

Saucy Vegetables

Make every meal-time an adventure. Begin your quest here by sampling our delicious duo of vegetables and white sauce. Each one of these recipes is a taste sensation worth exploring.

The route is easy—just start the vegetables cooking. As they cook, prepare the rich and creamy white sauce. You'll know your search has paid off at first bite!

Cheesy Brussels Sprouts and Tofu

Cheesy Brussels Sprouts and Tofu

A meatless main dish that's just right for lunch or a light supper.

10	ounces (275g) fresh or frozen brussels sprouts
2	tablespoons butter *or* margarine
1	tablespoon plain flour
⅛	teaspoon salt
	Dash pepper
6	fluid ounces (150ml) milk
4	ounces (110ml) grated processed cheese
2	tablespoons chopped pimento
¼	teaspoon bottled hot pepper sauce
8	ounces (225g) tofu (fresh bean curd), cut into ½-inch (1cm) cubes
	Chow mein noodles
1½	ounces (40g) chopped peanuts

Trim stems, remove wilted leaves, and wash fresh brussels sprouts. Cut large sprouts in half. In a medium saucepan bring a small amount of lightly salted water to boiling. Add fresh brussels sprouts. Return to boiling; reduce heat. Cook, covered, for 13 to 15 minutes or until crisp-tender (see photo 1). Drain. (*Or,* cook frozen brussels sprouts according to packet directions; drain.)

Meanwhile, make sauce. In a medium saucepan melt butter or margarine. Stir in flour, salt, and pepper (see photo 2). Add milk all at once (see photo 3). Cook and stir until thickened and bubbly, then cook and stir 1 minute more (see photo 4). Add cheese, pimento, and hot pepper sauce; stir until cheese is melted.

Gently stir brussels sprouts and tofu into sauce. Heat through. Transfer mixture to a serving bowl. Serve over chow mein noodles. Sprinkle peanuts on top of each serving. Makes 4 main-dish servings.

Microwave Directions: In a microwave-safe casserole combine fresh or frozen brussels sprouts and 2 tablespoons *water*. Micro-cook, covered, on 100% power (HIGH) 3 to 5 minutes for fresh or 7 to 9 minutes for frozen, or until crisp-tender, stirring once. Drain. In a 32-fluid-ounce (900ml) glass measuring jug cook butter or margarine, uncovered, on high 30 to 60 seconds. Stir in flour, salt, and pepper (see photo 2). Add milk all at once (see photo 3). Cook on high 2 to 3 minutes or until thick and bubbly, stirring *every* minute. Stir in cheese, pimento, and hot pepper sauce until cheese is melted. Add sauce to brussels sprouts in casserole. Gently stir in tofu. Cook, uncovered, on high about 2 minutes or until heated through, stirring mixture once. Serve as above.

1 Wait until you've added the vegetables to the boiling water, returned the water to boiling, and adjusted the heat so the water is just simmering. Then cover the pan and start timing the cooking.

2 Stir the flour into the melted butter or margarine until the mixture is well combined with no lumps. Combining the ingredients thoroughly at this point makes it easier to prevent lumps when the liquid is added.

Select a wooden spoon. The handle stays cool and makes it more comfortable to stir.

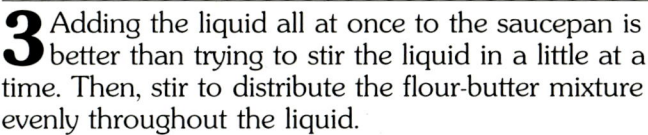

3 Adding the liquid all at once to the saucepan is better than trying to stir the liquid in a little at a time. Then, stir to distribute the flour-butter mixture evenly throughout the liquid.

4 Stir the mixture constantly in a figure-8 motion so it is evenly heated and does not stick to the bottom of the pan. If you stir too vigorously, the sauce will not be smooth and velvety.

Creamy Caraway Cabbage

Traditional flavours of a German menu—cabbage, caraway, rye, and mustard—all rolled into one dish.

20 ounces (550g) shredded cabbage
 6 ounces (175g) sliced fresh mushrooms
 2 ounces (50g) sliced spring onion
 1 tablespoon butter *or* margarine
 1 tablespoon plain flour
 ⅛ teaspoon pepper
 4 fluid ounces (110ml) milk
 8 ounces (225g) soured cream
 2 tablespoons plain flour
 2 teaspoons prepared mustard
 ½ teaspoon caraway seed
 3 ounces (75g) crushed rye crackers
   (optional)

In a large saucepan bring a small amount of lightly salted water to boiling. Add cabbage, mushrooms, and onion. Return to boiling; reduce heat. Cook, covered, about 7 minutes or until crisp-tender (see photo 1, page 68). Drain; return to saucepan.

Meanwhile, make sauce. In a small saucepan melt butter or margarine. Stir in 1 tablespoon flour and pepper (see photo 2, page 69). Add milk all at once (see photo 3, page 69). Cook and stir until thickened and bubbly (see photo 4, page 69).

In a small bowl combine soured cream, 2 tablespoons flour, mustard, and caraway seed. Add to sauce in small saucepan. Cook and stir until thickened and bubbly, cook and stir 1 minute more. Add soured cream sauce to cabbage mixture; stir until coated. Heat through. Transfer mixture to serving dish. Top with crushed rye crackers, if desired. Makes 4 servings.

Beer-Cheese Broccoli and Onion

The robust flavour of this beer-and-cheese sauce is also good with cauliflower, celeriac, or a combination of cauliflower and broccoli.

1 pound (450g) broccoli
1 large onion, cut into thin wedges
2 tablespoons butter *or* margarine
2 tablespoons plain flour
⅛ teaspoon pepper
6 fluid ounces (165ml) milk
3 ounces (75g) grated processed cheese
2 fluid ounces (55ml) beer

Wash broccoli; remove outer leaves and tough parts of stalks. Cut off florets; set aside. Chop stems into 1- to 1½-inch (2.5 to 4cm) pieces. In a medium saucepan bring a small amount of lightly salted water to boiling. Add chopped broccoli stems and onion. Return to boiling; reduce heat. Cook, covered, for 5 minutes (see photo 1, page 68). Add florets and cook 5 minutes more or until broccoli is crisp-tender; drain well and set aside.

Meanwhile, in a medium saucepan melt butter or margarine. Stir in flour and pepper (see photo 2, page 69). Add milk all at once (see photo 3, page 69). Cook and stir until thickened and bubbly, then cook and stir 1 minute more (see photo 4, page 69). Add cheese and beer; stir until cheese is melted. Stir in drained broccoli and onion. Heat through. Makes 6 servings.

Cauliflower Supreme

Rich and creamy, thanks to the Parmesan cheese and cream cheese.

6 ounces (175g) cauliflower florets
8 ounces (225g) sliced celery
4 ounces (110g) chopped onion
4 ounces (110g) chopped sweet red *or* green pepper
2 tablespoons butter *or* margarine
2 tablespoons plain flour
¼ teaspoon salt
⅛ teaspoon pepper
8 fluid ounces (220ml) milk
3 ounces (75g) cream cheese, cut up
2 tablespoons fine dry bread crumbs
2 tablespoons grated Parmesan cheese
1 tablespoon butter *or* margarine, melted

In a medium saucepan bring a small amount of lightly salted water to boiling. Add cauliflower, celery, onion, and red or green pepper. Return to boiling; reduce heat. Cook, covered, 5 to 7 minutes or until crisp-tender (*see photo 1, page 68*). Drain.

To make sauce, in a medium saucepan melt 2 tablespoons butter or margarine. Stir in flour, salt, and pepper (*see photo 2, page 69*). Add milk all at once (*see photo 3, page 69*). Cook and stir until thick and bubbly, then cook and stir 1 minute more (*see photo 4, page 69*).

Add cream cheese to sauce; stir until cheese is melted. Stir in drained vegetable mixture. Heat through. In a small bowl combine bread crumbs, Parmesan cheese, and 1 tablespoon melted butter or margarine. Transfer vegetable mixture to a serving bowl. Top with bread crumb mixture. Makes 6 servings.

Swiss Cheese and Bacon Potatoes

Our Test Kitchen found red potatoes hold their shape better than other potatoes for this type of dish.

1⅓ pounds (600g) potatoes (4 medium)
2 ounces (50g) chopped onion
2 tablespoons butter *or* margarine
2 tablespoons plain flour
⅛ teaspoon ground nutmeg
⅛ teaspoon pepper
12 fluid ounces (330ml) milk
3 ounces (75g) processed Swiss cheese
6 rashers streaky bacon, crisp-cooked, drained, and crumbled

Wash and peel potatoes. In a large saucepan bring a moderate amount of lightly salted water to boiling. Add whole potatoes. Return to boiling; reduce heat. Cook, covered, about 30 minutes or until tender (*see photo 1, page 68*). Drain and cool slightly. Cut potatoes into thin slices; return potatoes to the saucepan.

Meanwhile, make sauce. In a small saucepan cook onion in hot butter or margarine until tender but not brown. Stir in flour, nutmeg, and pepper (*see photo 2, page 69*). Add milk all at once (*see photo 3, page 69*). Cook and stir until thickened and bubbly, then cook and stir 1 minute more (*see photo 4, page 69*).

Add cheese to sauce; stir until cheese is melted. Add cheese sauce and *half* of the streaky bacon to potatoes; stir gently until potatoes are coated. Heat through. Transfer mixture to a serving dish. Sprinkle with remaining streaky bacon. Makes 6 to 8 servings.

Classy Cream Soups

Ooh, là là! We've put a little bit of France into every soup in this chapter.

From across the Channel, we borrowed the French cooking technique of pureeing to give these soups their smooth, creamy texture.

So sit back and enjoy the taste of these rich, velvety soups. Each one is a love affair of flavours you'll want to experience firsthand. *Bon appétit!*

Chilled Spinach Soup

Chilled Spinach Soup

A cold, tangy soup starts any meal off on the right note.

14½ **fluid ounces (400ml) tinned chicken broth**
2 **ounces (50g) chopped onion**
1 **clove garlic, minced**
8 **ounces (225g) torn spinach *or* 10-ounces (275g) frozen chopped spinach**
1 **ounce (25g) cornflour**
6 **fluid ounces (165ml) single cream *or* milk**
8 **ounces (225g) natural yogurt**
  Natural yogurt (optional)
  Lemon slices, halved (optional)
  Mint leaves (optional)

In a medium saucepan combine *half* of the broth, onion, and garlic. Bring to boiling. Add torn spinach. Return to boiling; reduce heat. Cook, covered, for 3 to 5 minutes or until spinach is tender. (*Or,* if using frozen spinach, cook for 8 to 10 minutes or until tender.) *Do not drain.*

In a food processor bowl or blender container place undrained spinach mixture. Cover; process or blend until smooth (see photo 1).

In the same saucepan combine remaining chicken broth and cornflour; add spinach mixture. Cook and stir until thickened and bubbly, then cook and stir 2 minutes more. Remove from heat. Stir in single cream or milk (see photo 2). Transfer spinach soup to a bowl. Cover and chill thoroughly.

Add yogurt to soup. Using a wire whisk or rotary beater, mix thoroughly (see photo 3). Ladle into 4 soup bowls. If desired, garnish each serving with some additional yogurt; swirl lightly (see photo, pages 72–73). Garnish with lemon slices and mint leaves, if desired. Serves 4.

1 Process the spinach mixture until the entire mixture is smooth or pureed. Stop the machine occasionally and scrape the sides of the container to move the food back toward the blades.

2 Stir the single cream or milk into vegetable mixture after it is pureed. Single cream adds richness to the soup. For about 30 calories less per serving, use milk.

3 Gently stir the yogurt into the soup until the two mixtures are well mixed. A wire whisk is especially good for breaking up the yogurt, but a rotary beater or a spoon also works.

Autumnfest Soup

Our food editors sampled this soup on taste panel and unanimously declared it "Outstanding!"

1½	**pounds (700g) acorn squash (1 medium)**
16	**fluid ounces (425ml) tinned chicken broth**
⅛	**teaspoon salt**
⅛	**teaspoon ground nutmeg**
	Dash pepper
8	**fluid ounces (220ml) single cream *or* milk**

Halve squash; remove seeds. Cut each piece in half. Place steamer basket in a large saucepan; add broth to saucepan. Bring broth to boiling; place squash in steamer basket. Cover and steam for 25 to 30 minutes or until squash can be pierced easily with fork. Carefully remove steamer basket from saucepan (see photo 5, page 41). Reserve steaming liquid in saucepan.

Using a spoon, scoop squash pulp out of peel; discard peel. Place pulp in a food processor bowl or blender container. Cover; process or blend until smooth, adding small amounts of the reserved liquid as necessary (see photo 1, page 74).

Stir squash into reserved liquid in the saucepan; stir in salt, nutmeg, and pepper. Bring mixture to boiling; reduce heat. Stir in cream or milk (see photo 2, page 74). Heat through. Serve immediately. Makes 4 servings.

Creamy Pea Soup

10	**ounces (275g) fresh or frozen peas**
14½	**ounces (400ml) tinned chicken broth**
2	**ounces (50g) lettuce *or* spinach**
4	**ounces (110g) chopped onion**
½	**teaspoon lemon pepper**
6	**fluid ounces (165ml) single cream *or* milk**
	Croutons (optional)

In a medium saucepan combine peas, broth, lettuce or spinach, onion, and lemon pepper.

Bring to boiling; reduce heat. Simmer, covered, for 10 to 15 minutes or until peas are very tender.

In a food processor bowl or blender container place *half* of the pea mixture. Cover and process or blend until smooth (see photo 1, page 74). Transfer smooth pea mixture to a mixing bowl. Repeat with remaining pea mixture.

Return pea mixtures to the saucepan. Stir in cream or milk (see photo 2, page 74). Heat through. Ladle into soup bowls. Sprinkle croutons on top of soup, if desired. Serves 4 to 6.

Cheesy Mushroom Soup

2	**ounces (50g) butter *or* margarine**
6	**ounces (175g) chopped fresh mushrooms**
2	**tablespoons plain flour**
8	**fluid ounces (220ml) tinned chicken broth**
8	**fluid ounces (220ml) single cream *or* milk**
½	**teaspoon dried basil, crushed**
3	**ounces (75g) cream cheese, cut up**
	Sliced fresh mushrooms (optional)

In a medium saucepan melt butter or margarine; add mushrooms. Cover and cook over medium heat about 7 minutes or until tender.

In a food processor bowl or blender container place mushroom mixture and flour. Cover; process or blend until smooth (see photo 1, page 74).

Return mushroom mixture to the saucepan. Stir in broth, cream or milk, basil, and dash *pepper* (see photo 2, page 74). Cook and stir until thickened and bubbly. Cook and stir 1 minute more. Reduce heat. Add cream cheese; cook and stir until cheese is melted. Ladle into 4 soup bowls. Sprinkle with mushroom slices and snipped parsley, if desired. Makes 4 servings.

Broccoli-Cheese Soup

Here you skip the step of grating the cheese. Instead, your food processor or blender grates it while pureeing the soup.

10 ounces (275g) fresh or frozen broccoli
14½ fluid ounces (400ml) tinned chicken broth
1 clove garlic, minced
Dash pepper
4 ounces (110g) cubed processed Swiss cheese
2 tablespoons plain flour
12 fluid ounces (330ml) single cream *or* milk
Soured cream (optional)

In a medium saucepan combine broccoli, chicken broth, garlic, and pepper. Bring to boiling; reduce heat. Simmer, covered, about 15 minutes or until broccoli is very tender. *Do not drain.*

In a food processor bowl or blender container place *half* of the broccoli mixture. Cover; process or blend until smooth (see photo 1, page 74). Pour mixture into a bowl. Add remaining broccoli mixture to the food processor bowl or blender. Cover; process or blend until smooth. Add cheese and flour. Cover and process or blend until smooth.

Return broccoli mixtures to the saucepan. Stir in single cream or milk (see photo 2, page 74). Cook and stir until thickened and bubbly. Cook and stir 1 minute more. Ladle soup into 4 soup bowls. Dollop with some soured cream, if desired. Makes 4 main-dish servings.

Hearty Potato Soup

Adding a little ham or clams rounds out the flavour of the potatoes.

4 medium potatoes, peeled and chopped
14½ fluid ounces (400ml) tinned chicken broth
1 small onion, chopped
¼ teaspoon salt
¼ teaspoon dried basil, crushed
Dash pepper
12 fluid ounces (330ml) single cream *or* milk
1 tablespoon plain flour
4 ounces (110g) finely minced fully cooked ham *or* 6½ ounces (185g) tinned clams in brine, drained and minced
2 ounces (50g) grated carrot

In a medium saucepan combine potatoes, chicken broth, onion, salt, basil, and pepper. Bring to boiling; reduce heat. Simmer, covered, for 10 to 15 minutes or until potatoes are tender. *Do not drain.*

In a food processor bowl or blender container place *half* of the potato mixture. Cover; process or blend until smooth (see photo 1, page 74). Transfer mixture to a mixing bowl. Repeat for remaining potato mixture.

Return potato mixtures to the saucepan. Combine single cream or milk and flour; stir into potato mixture (see photo 2, page 74). Cook and stir until thickened and bubbly. Stir in ham or drained clams and grated carrot. Cook and stir until heated through. Makes 4 main-dish servings.

Hearty Dry Bean Dishes

Q. I'm looking for a hot and hearty dish that's simple to make, yet deliciously homemade. Any ideas?

A. Yes! Make your family a tasty bean dish—they're satisfying and easy to prepare. Just toss dry beans into a pot of water, add a couple of other ingredients, then sit back and let them cook.

Any one of these recipes will fill up your tummy and warm you right down to your toes.

Vegetarian Chilli

Vegetarian Chilli

A vegetable lover's dream come true—a meatless chilli with a nice, hot kick.

4 ounces (110ml) dry red kidney beans
4 ounces (110ml) dry haricot beans
14½ fluid ounces (400ml) tinned chicken broth
28 ounces (810g) tinned tomatoes, cut up
8 ounces (225g) chopped celery (2 stalks)
8 ounces (225g) chopped onion (1 medium)
8 fluid ounces (220ml) beer
4 ounces (110g) tinned diced green chilli peppers, drained
1 tablespoon chilli powder
1 tablespoon snipped parsley
1 teaspoon dried basil, crushed
1 teaspoon dried oregano, crushed
2 cloves garlic, minced
¼ teaspoon pepper
4 ounces (110g) grated processed cheese
3 ounces (75g) unsalted peanuts, coarsely chopped, *or* sunflower nuts

Rinse dry beans. In a large saucepan combine beans and 24 fluid ounces (680ml) *water* (see photo 1). Bring to boiling; reduce heat. Simmer 2 minutes. Remove from heat. Cover; let stand 1 hour. (*Or*, soak beans in water overnight.)

Drain beans in a colander and rinse, discarding liquid (see photo 2). Return beans to the saucepan. Add chicken broth. Bring to boiling; reduce heat. Simmer, covered, about 1 hour or until beans are tender (see photo 3).

Stir in *undrained* tomatoes, celery, onion, beer, green chilli peppers, chilli powder, parsley, basil, oregano, garlic, and pepper. Return to boiling; reduce heat. Simmer, covered, for 45 minutes.

Uncover and simmer 15 minutes more or to desired consistency, stirring occasionally. Ladle into 4 soup bowls. Sprinkle cheese and peanuts or sunflower nuts on top of soup. Makes 4 main-dish servings.

1 Add the specified amount of cold water to the rinsed dry beans (usually about three times the amount of the beans).

2 Pour the soaked beans into a colander, *discarding* the soaking liquid. Then rinse the beans thoroughly under running tap water.

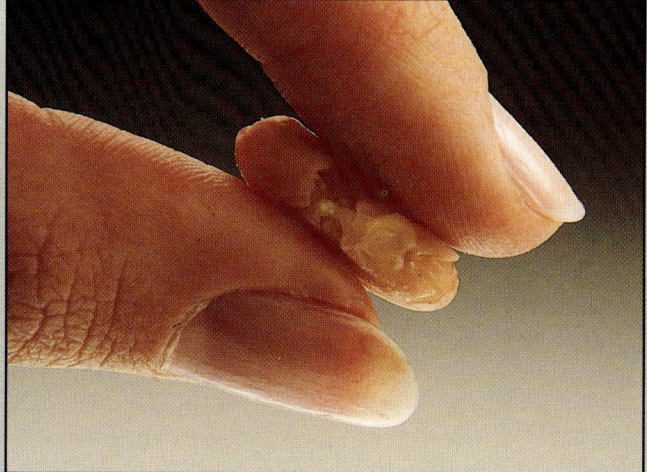

3 Remove a few beans from the saucepan and press the beans between your thumb and finger. The beans are tender when they feel soft. If there is a hard core, cook a little longer, testing them again frequently.

New England Baked Beans

½ pound (225g) dry haricot beans
4 ounces (110g) chopped belly pork *or*
    4 rashers streaky bacon, cut up
4 ounces (110g) chopped onion
    (1 medium)
2 fluid ounces (55ml) black treacle
2 tablespoons soft brown sugar
1 teaspoon mustard powder
⅛ teaspoon salt
⅛ teaspoon pepper

Rinse dry beans. In a saucepan combine beans and 32 fluid ounces (900ml) *water* (see photo 1, page 81). Bring to boiling; reduce heat. Simmer for 2 minutes. Remove from heat. Cover; let stand 1 hour. (*Or,* soak beans overnight.)

Drain beans in a colander and rinse, discarding liquid (see photo 2, page 81). Return to saucepan; add 22 fluid ounces (645ml) fresh *water* and ¼ teaspoon *salt*. Bring to boiling; reduce heat. Simmer, covered, 1¼ to 1½ hours or until beans are tender (see photo 3, page 81).

Drain beans, reserving *4 fluid ounces (110ml)* liquid. In a medium casserole combine beans, reserved liquid, meat, onion, black treacle, soft brown sugar, mustard, salt, and pepper.

Bake, covered, in a 300°F (150°C) gas mark 2 oven for 1 hour. Bake, uncovered, for 30 minutes more or to desired consistency, stirring occasionally. Serves 6.

Overnight Soaking

Soaking dry beans is simple. Rinse the beans and place them in a bowl with the specified amount of cold water. Cover and set in a cool place 6 to 8 hours or overnight.

Herbed Bean Stew

8 ounces (225g) dry haricot beans
6 ounces (175g) dry red kidney beans
8 ounces (225g) chopped onion (1 large)
2 cloves garlic, minced
2 bay leaves
10 ounces (275g) chopped, peeled turnip
8 ounces (225g) tinned, sieved tomatoes
2 tablespoons plain flour
1½ teaspoons instant beef bouillon
    granules
1 teaspoon caster sugar
1 teaspoon dried oregano, crushed
10 ounces (275g) frozen French
    beans, thawed
1 packet shortcrust pastry mix
3 ounces (75g) grated cheddar cheese
2 tablespoons toasted wheat germ

Rinse dry beans. In a 128-fluid-ounce (3.6l) covered casserole combine beans and 48 fluid ounces (1.4l) *water* (see photo 1, page 81). Bring to boiling; reduce heat. Simmer for 2 minutes. Remove from heat. Cover; let stand 1 hour. (*Or,* soak beans in water overnight.)

Drain beans and rinse, discarding liquid (see photo 2, page 81). Return to the pan. Add onion, garlic, bay leaves, 36 fluid ounces (1110ml) fresh *water,* and 1 teaspoon *salt*. Bring to boiling; reduce heat. Simmer, covered, 1¼ hours or until tender.

Add turnip; cook 20 to 30 minutes or until tender. Drain, reserving 8 fluid ounces (220ml) liquid. Discard bay leaves. In a large casserole combine sieved tomatoes, flour, bouillon granules, sugar, oregano, and ¼ teaspoon *pepper*. Add bean mixture, reserved liquid, and French beans.

In a bowl combine pastry mix, cheese, and wheat germ. Prepare crust according to packet directions; roll dough into a circle 2 inches (5cm) larger than casserole top. Place crust atop casserole; turn edge under and flute to sides of casserole. Cut slits in crust. Bake in a 400°F (200°C) gas mark 6 oven 20 to 25 minutes or until golden. Makes 6 main-dish servings.

Black Beans and Rice

A tradition borrowed from the Caribbean and South American countries—black beans and rice served with a host of toppings.

½ pound (225g) dry black beans
1 pound (450g) smoked pork hocks (2 to 3)
14½ fluid ounces (400ml) tinned beef broth
4 ounces (110g) chopped onion (1 medium)
2 cloves garlic, minced
2 bay leaves
¼ teaspoon pepper
1 tablespoon vinegar
  Hot cooked rice
  Soured cream (optional)
  Sliced spring onion (optional)
  Sliced radishes (optional)
  Cooked peas (optional)
  Lime wedges (optional)

Rinse dry beans. In a large saucepan combine beans and 32 fluid ounces (900ml) *water* (see photo 1, page 81). Bring to boiling; reduce heat. Simmer for 2 minutes. Remove from heat. Cover; let stand 1 hour. (*Or,* soak beans overnight.)

Drain beans in a colander and rinse, discarding liquid (see photo 2, page 81). Return beans to the saucepan. Add pork hocks, beef broth, onion, garlic, bay leaves, pepper, and 4 fluid ounces (110ml) fresh *water.* Bring to boiling; reduce heat. Simmer, covered, about 2 hours or until beans are tender (see photo 3, page 81).

Remove and discard bay leaves. Remove pork hocks. When hocks are cool enough to handle, cut off meat and dice. Discard bones. Add diced meat and vinegar to bean mixture. Season to taste with *salt* and *pepper.* Heat and serve over hot cooked rice. Serve soured cream, spring onion, radishes, peas, and lime wedges with beans, if desired. Makes 4 main-dish servings.

Minestrone

Jalapeño pepper in the cheese adds zing to the soup.

6 ounces (175g) dry haricot beans *or* pinto beans
21 fluid ounces (600ml) tinned condensed beef broth
2 bay leaves
½ teaspoon dried basil, crushed
½ teaspoon dried oregano, crushed
2 cloves garlic, minced
6 ounces (175g) French beans, cut into 1-inch (2.5cm) pieces, *or* frozen cut French beans
4 ounces (110g) chopped onion (1 medium)
2 ounces (50g) diced carrots
3 ounces (75g) spaghetti, broken into 2-inch (5cm) pieces
2 ounces (50g) grated Gouda cheese *or* Monterey Jack cheese with jalapeño peppers

Rinse dry beans. In a 128-fluid-ounce (1.4l) covered casserole combine beans and 32 fluid ounces (900ml) *water* (see photo 1, page 81). Bring to boiling; reduce heat. Simmer for 2 minutes. Remove from heat. Cover; let stand 1 hour. (*Or,* soak beans in water overnight.)

Drain beans in a colander and rinse, discarding liquid (see photo 2, page 81). Return beans to the casserole. Add beef broth, bay leaves, basil, oregano, garlic, and 20 fluid ounces (570ml) fresh *water.* Bring to boiling; reduce heat. Simmer, covered, for 1 to 1¼ hours or until beans are tender (see photo 3, page 81).

Remove and discard bay leaves. Stir in French beans, onion, and carrots. Simmer, covered, for 10 minutes. Stir in spaghetti. Return to boiling; reduce heat. Cook, covered, 15 to 20 minutes more or until vegetables are tender. Ladle soup into 4 soup bowls. Sprinkle cheese on top of soup. Makes 4 main-dish servings.

Say It with A Stir-Fry

When you want the message to be great taste, let a stir-fry say it all.

With stir-frying, you always use a direct connection. The high heat quickly cooks the vegetables, letting them retain maximum flavour and freshness.

Whether it's a main dish or a side dish, the delicious delivery comes across loud and clear.

Cauliflower-Asparagus Stir-Fry

Cauliflower-Asparagus Stir-Fry

3/4 **pound (350g) asparagus *or* 10 ounces (275g) frozen cut asparagus, thawed**
1/4 **teaspoon finely grated orange peel**
3 **fluid ounces (80ml) orange juice**
1 **teaspoon cornflour**
1/4 **teaspoon ground ginger**
1 **tablespoon cooking oil**
4 1/2 **ounces (125g) thinly sliced cauliflower florets**
2 **tablespoons slivered almonds, toasted**

Wash fresh asparagus and scrape off scales, if desired. Break off woody bases; discard. Bias-slice asparagus into 1- or 2-inch (2.5 or 5cm) pieces. Set aside. For sauce, in a small bowl stir together orange peel, orange juice, cornflour, ginger, and 1/8 teaspoon *salt.* Set aside.

Preheat a wok or large frying pan over high heat; add oil (see photo 1). Stir-fry cauliflower for 1 minute, then add asparagus and stir-fry about 4 minutes or until vegetables are crisp-tender (see photo 2). Push vegetables from centre of the wok or frying pan (see photo 3).

Stir sauce; add to centre of wok or frying pan. Cook and stir until thickened and bubbly, then cook and stir for 30 seconds more. Stir vegetables into sauce until coated (see photo 4). Sprinkle with almonds. Makes 4 servings.

1 Drizzle the oil near the top of the hot wok, as shown. The oil coats the wok as it runs toward the centre. If using a frying pan add oil, then lift and tilt to coat cooking surface.

2 To stir-fry, use a long-handled wooden spoon or spatula to lift and turn the vegetables in a folding motion. Keep the food moving all the time for even cooking.

3 Make room to cook the sauce by pushing the vegetables away from the centre of the wok or frying pan.

4 When the sauce is completely cooked, stir the vegetables back toward the centre of the wok or frying pan. Then toss until all of the vegetables are coated with the sauce.

Sweet 'n' Sour Vegetables

Crisp shredded cabbage and mange tout in an apple-flavoured sweet and sour sauce.

3 **ounces (75g) fresh mange tout *or* frozen mange tout, thawed**
3 **fluid ounces (80ml) apple juice**
2 **tablespoons wine vinegar**
1 **tablespoon soft brown sugar**
1½ **teaspoons cornflour**
1 **tablespoon cooking oil**
12 **ounces (350g) shredded cabbage**
10 **ounces (275g) halved fresh mushrooms**

Wash fresh mange tout; cut ends and remove strings, if necessary. For sauce, in a small bowl stir together apple juice, wine vinegar, soft brown sugar, and cornflour. Set aside.

Preheat a wok or large frying pan over high heat; add cooking oil (see photo 1, page 86). Stir-fry cabbage in hot oil for 2 minutes (see photo 2, page 87). Add more cooking oil as necessary. Add mange tout and mushrooms. Stir-fry 2 minutes more. Push vegetables from the centre of the wok or frying pan (see photo 3, page 87).

Stir sauce; add to centre of wok or frying pan. Cook and stir until thickened and bubbly, then cook and stir 1 minute more. Stir vegetables into sauce until coated (see photo 4, page 87). Serve immediately. Makes 4 servings.

Curried Vegetables

An attractive array of vegetables—carrots, brussels sprouts, and red or green pepper—in a golden curry sauce.

2 **ounces (50g) fresh brussels sprouts *or* frozen brussels sprouts, thawed**
4 **fluid ounces (110ml) tinned chicken broth**
2 **fluid ounces (55ml) dry white wine**
4 **teaspoons cornflour**
2 **teaspoons caster sugar**
2 **teaspoons curry powder**
1 **tablespoon cooking oil**
4 **ounces (110g) carrots, sliced (2 medium) (see photo 2, page 8)**
1 **medium sweet red *or* green pepper, cut into bite-size strips**
2 **tablespoons thinly sliced spring onion**
4 **ounces (110g) tofu (fresh bean curd), cut into ½-inch (1cm) cubes**
2½ **ounces (60g) peanuts**
Hot cooked bulgur *or* rice

Cut brussels sprouts in half. In a saucepan cook brussels sprouts in a small amount of boiling salted water for 5 minutes. Drain; set aside.

For sauce, in a small bowl stir together chicken broth, wine, cornflour, sugar, curry powder, and ¼ teaspoon *salt.* Set mixture aside.

Preheat a wok or large frying pan over high heat; add cooking oil (see photo 1, page 86). Stir-fry carrots in hot oil for 1 minute (see photo 2, page 87). Add more oil as necessary. Add brussels sprouts. Stir-fry for 3 minutes; add red or green pepper and onion. Stir-fry 1 minute more. Push vegetables from the centre of the wok or frying pan (see photo 3, page 87).

Stir sauce; add to the centre of the wok or frying pan. Cook and stir until thickened and bubbly, then cook and stir 1 minute more. Stir vegetables into sauce until coated (see photo 4, page 87). Add tofu. Cover and cook about 30 seconds or until heated through. Stir in peanuts. Serve immediately over hot cooked bulgur or rice. Makes 4 main-dish servings.

Dilled French Beans And Tomatoes

The soured-cream-dill sauce is great with either French beans or asparagus.

6 ounces (175g) French beans *or* asparagus
2 fluid ounces (55ml) water
½ teaspoon instant chicken bouillon granules
4 ounces (110g) soured cream
2 teaspoons cornflour
½ teaspoon dried dill
1 tablespoon cooking oil
1 medium tomato, seeded and chopped

Remove ends and strings from beans. Slice beans into 1-inch (2.5cm) pieces. Cook, covered, in a small amount of boiling lightly salted water for 4 minutes; drain well. (*Or,* wash asparagus and scrape off scales, if desired. Break off and discard woody bases. Bias-slice asparagus into 1-inch [2.5cm] pieces.)

For sauce, in a small bowl combine water and bouillon granules; stir to dissolve. Stir in soured cream, cornflour, and dill. Set aside.

Preheat a wok or large frying pan over high heat; add cooking oil (*see* photo 1, page 86). Stir-fry French beans or asparagus in hot oil for 3 to 5 minutes or until crisp-tender (*see* photo 2, page 87). Push vegetables from the centre of the wok or frying pan (*see* photo 3, page 87). Reduce heat.

Add sauce to centre of the wok or frying pan. Cook and stir until thickened and bubbly, then cook and stir for 1 minute more. Stir in beans or asparagus. Add tomato; stir vegetables gently into sauce until coated (*see* photo 4, page 87). Serve immediately. Makes 6 servings.

Chayote-Rice Stir-Fry

Chilling the rice keeps it from sticking to the hot wok.

1 tablespoon cooking oil
½ pound (225g) cubed, peeled, seeded chayote (about 1 medium) *or* cubed courgette (about 2 medium)
3 ounces (75g) sliced fresh mushrooms
1 small onion, thinly sliced
1 small green pepper, cut into bite-size strips
1 clove garlic, minced
12 ounces (350g) cooked rice, chilled
4 ounces (110g) fresh bean sprouts
1 tablespoon soy sauce
2 ounces (55g) grated cheddar cheese

Preheat a wok or large frying pan over high heat; add cooking oil (*see* photo 1, page 86). Stir-fry cubed chayote or courgette in hot oil for 3 to 4 minutes or until almost crisp-tender (*see* photo 2, page 87).

Add more oil to the wok or frying pan as necessary. Add mushrooms, onion, green pepper, and garlic. Stir-fry 3 to 4 minutes more or until all vegetables are crisp-tender. Stir in chilled rice, bean sprouts, and soy sauce. Heat through. Transfer to a serving bowl; sprinkle with cheese. Serve immediately. Makes 4 to 6 servings.

Stir-Frying Without a Wok

Ready to try your hand at stir-frying, but you don't own a wok? No problem. You don't need one to stir-fry like a pro. All that's required is a large, deep frying pan. The high sides on the frying pan make it easy to stir and toss the foods without making a mess.

Pork and Pepper Stir-Fry

A nifty trick from our Test Kitchen—it's easier to slice very thin strips if you put the meat in the freezer for 45 minutes until it's partially frozen.

1 **pound (450g) boneless pork**
2 **fluid ounces (55ml) water**
2 **tablespoons soy sauce**
2 **teaspoons cornflour**
¼ **teaspoon ground ginger**
 Several dashes bottled hot pepper sauce
1 **tablespoon cooking oil**
2 **medium green peppers, cut into strips**
1 **small onion, cut into thin wedges**
2⅔ **ounces halved cherry tomatoes**

Partially freeze pork. Cut pork across the grain into very thin bite-size strips. For sauce, in a small bowl stir together water, soy sauce, cornflour, ginger, and hot pepper sauce. Set aside.

Preheat a wok or large frying pan over high heat; add cooking oil (see photo 1, page 86). Stir-fry green peppers and onion in hot oil about 2 minutes or until crisp-tender (see photo 2, page 87). Remove vegetables from the wok or frying pan.

Add more oil to the wok or frying pan as necessary. Add *half* of the pork to the wok or frying pan. Stir-fry about 3 minutes or until pork is no longer pink. Remove pork. Stir-fry remaining pork about 3 minutes. Return all pork to the wok or frying pan. Push pork from the centre of the wok or frying pan (see photo 3, page 87).

Stir sauce; add to the centre of the wok or frying pan. Cook and stir until thickened and bubbly, then cook and stir 1 minute more. Return vegetables to the wok or frying pan; add tomatoes. Stir pork and vegetables into sauce until coated (see photo 4, page 87). Cover and cook for 1 minute. Serve immediately. Makes 4 main-dish servings.

◄ Cantonese Beef with Hoisin Sauce

Cantonese Beef With Hoisin Sauce

1 **pound (450g) boneless beef sirloin steak**
2 **fluid ounces (55ml) soy sauce**
2 **tablespoons dry sherry**
2 **tablespoons hoisin sauce**
2 **teaspoons sugar**
¾ **teaspoon sesame oil**
⅛ **teaspoon whole aniseed**
1 **tablespoon cornflour**
8 **ounces (225g) fresh mange tout**
3 **tablespoons cooking oil**
16 **ounces (450g) broccoli florets**
3 **medium carrots, thinly sliced**
4 **ounces (110g) sliced spring onions**
3 **ounces (75g) cashews**

Partially freeze beef. Cut beef across the grain into very thin bite-size strips. In a large bowl stir together soy sauce, sherry, hoisin sauce, sugar, sesame oil, and aniseed. Stir in beef strips. Cover; chill for 2 to 3 hours, stirring occasionally.

In a bowl combine cornflour and 4 fluid ounces (110ml) cold *water*. Drain beef; reserve marinade. Wash mange tout; cut ends and remove strings. Set aside.

Preheat a wok or large frying pan over high heat; add *1 tablespoon* cooking oil (see photo 1, page 86). Stir-fry broccoli and carrots in hot oil for 4 minutes (see photo 2, page 87). Add mange tout and spring onions; stir-fry 2 minutes more. Remove vegetables from the wok or frying pan.

Add *1 tablespoon* oil. Stir-fry *half* of the beef for 2 to 3 minutes or until done. Remove beef from the wok. Add remaining oil as necessary. Stir-fry remaining beef for 2 to 3 minutes or until done. Return all beef to the wok. Push beef from the centre of the wok (see photo 3, page 87).

Stir cornflour mixture. Add it and reserved marinade to the wok. Cook and stir until thickened and bubbly, then cook 1 minute more. Return vegetables to wok; stir beef and vegetables until coated (see photo 4, page 87). Heat through. Stir in cashews. Serve immediately with hot cooked rice, if desired. Makes 6 servings.

Great for Barbecuing

Ready to fire up for your next cook-out? Make it as relaxed and lazy as a summer day.

No reason to work up a sweat trying to get meat and vegetables ready at the same time. Let things slip into place by having the vegetables share the heat with the meat.

Ever so easy, these on-the-barbecue vegetables make any outdoor meal a real treat.

Kohl-Rabi Bake

Kohl-Rabi Bake

The German meaning for kohl-rabi describes the fla-vour—kohl means "cabbage" and rabi means "turnip."

¾ **pound (350g) small kohl-rabies**
1 **small onion, sliced**
1 **tablespoon butter *or* margarine**
2 **fluid ounces (55ml) chicken broth**
2 **ounces (50g) grated processed *or*
   cheddar cheese**
1 **tablespoon snipped parsley**

Peel kohl-rabies; cut into julienne strips (see photo 3, page 9). Cut an 18-inch (45cm) square of *heavy* silver foil (see photo 1). Place kohl-rabi and onion in centre of foil. Dot with butter or margarine; sprinkle with *pepper*. Fold up foil around kohl-rabi; add broth (see photo 2).

Bring up 2 opposite edges of foil and, leaving a little space for expansion of steam, seal tightly (see photo 3). Tightly seal each end also.

Place foil packet on a barbecue directly over *medium-hot* coals (see photo 4). Cook about 30 minutes or until kohl-rabi is tender. Remove from barbecue. Open packet; sprinkle with cheese and parsley. Serve with a slotted spoon. Makes 4 servings.

1 Measure the exact length of silver foil that the recipe calls for. *Heavy* foil makes a sturdy pack-et to hold the vegetables for barbecuing and is dis-posable for easy clean-up.

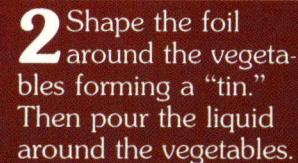

2 Shape the foil around the vegetables forming a "tin." Then pour the liquid around the vegetables.

3 Bring 2 opposite sides of the foil together and, leaving a little space for expansion of steam, fold over a ½-inch (1cm) seam. Then fold the seam again once or twice and press with your fingers to seal.

4 Hold your hand, palm side down, above the coals where the food will cook. Count the seconds, "one thousand one, one thousand two, etc." If you need to withdraw your hand after 2 seconds, the coals are *hot;* after 3 seconds, they're *medium-hot;* after 4 seconds, they're *medium;* and after 5 seconds, they're *medium-slow.*

Oriental Beans

2 tablespoons soy sauce
1 tablespoon water
⅛ teaspoon ground ginger
10½ ounces (285g) sliced French beans*
4 ounces (110g) sliced water chestnuts
1 tablespoon chopped pimento

In a small bowl combine soy sauce, water, and ginger. Cut an 18x12-inch (45x30cm) piece of *heavy* silver foil (see photo 1, page 94). Place French beans, water chestnuts, and pimento in centre of foil. Fold up foil around bean mixture; add soy sauce mixture (see photo 2, page 95).

Bring up long sides of foil and, leaving a little space for expansion of steam, seal tightly (see photo 3, page 95). Tightly seal each end also.

Place foil packet on a barbecue directly over *medium* coals (see photo 4, page 95). Cook for 25 to 30 minutes or until beans are crisp-tender, turning packet over once. Makes 4 servings.

*__Note:__ If desired, substitute 9 ounces (250g) *frozen cut French beans* for the fresh French beans. Prepare as above, *except* cook for 20 to 25 minutes, turning packet over once.

Barbecued Asparagus With Sorrel Dressing

Sorrel derives its name from the word "sour," which describes the tang of this spinach-like herb. If you want a milder flavour, substitute spinach.

2 ounces (50g) natural yogurt
2 ounces (50g) mayonnaise *or* salad dressing
½ ounce (10g) finely snipped sorrel *or* spinach
1 spring onion, finely chopped
1 pound (450g) asparagus
2 tablespoons water

For sorrel dressing, in a small bowl stir together yogurt, mayonnaise or salad dressing, sorrel or spinach, and spring onion. Cover and chill in the refrigerator.

Wash asparagus. Scrape off scales, if desired. Break off and discard bases. Cut an 18-inch (45cm) square of *heavy* silver foil (see photo 1, page 94). Place asparagus in the centre of the foil. Fold up foil around asparagus; add water (see photo 2, page 95).

Bring up 2 opposite edges of foil and, leaving a little space for expansion of steam, seal tightly (see photo 3, page 95). Tightly seal each end.

Place foil packet on a barbecue directly over *medium-hot* coals (see photo 4, page 95). Cook about 15 minutes or until asparagus is crisp-tender, turning packet over once. Serve immediately with sorrel dressing. Makes 4 servings.

Lemony Pepper Corn on the Cob

3 tablespoons butter *or* margarine, softened
1 teaspoon lemon pepper
1 teaspoon lemon juice
4 fresh corn on the cob
Paprika (optional)

In a small bowl stir together butter or margarine, lemon pepper, and lemon juice.

Remove husks and silk from the ears of corn. Cut two 18x12-inch (45x30cm) pieces of *heavy* silver foil (*see* photo 1, page 94). Cut each piece of foil in half to make four 12x9-inch (30x23cm) pieces.

Place 1 ear of corn in the centre of a piece of foil. Spread *one-quarter* of the butter mixture on the ear of corn. Bring up 2 long edges of foil and seal tightly (*see* photo 3, page 95). Tightly seal each end also. Repeat with remaining ears of corn.

Place corn on a barbecue, directly over *medium-hot* coals (*see* photo 4, page 95). Cook for 20 to 25 minutes or until tender, turning often. Sprinkle corn with paprika, if desired. Makes 4 servings.

Herbed Barbecued Potatoes

1¼ pounds (550g) potatoes (4 medium)
2 ounces (50g) butter *or* margarine, melted
2 tablespoons dry white wine
¼ teaspoon Italian seasoning

Cut potatoes *lengthwise* into quarters. In a large bowl combine melted butter or margarine, wine, and Italian seasoning. Add potatoes; toss to coat thoroughly.

Cut four 18x9-inch (45x23cm) pieces of *heavy* silver foil (*see* photo 1, page 94). Place 4 potato quarters in the centre of each piece of foil. Sprinkle potatoes with salt and pepper. Fold up foil around potatoes; drizzle with any remaining butter mixture (*see* photo 2, page 95).

For each packet, bring up 2 long edges of foil and, leaving a little space for expansion of steam, seal tightly (*see* photo 3, page 95). Tightly seal each end also.

Place foil packets on barbecue directly over *medium-hot* coals (*see* photo 4, page 95). Cook about 25 minutes or until tender. Serves 4.

Barbecued Beetroots

Mint jelly complements the flavour of the beetroots.

¾ pound (350g) beetroots (2 medium)
2 ounces (50g) mint jelly
1 tablespoon lemon juice
2 tablespoons butter *or* margarine

Wash beetroots; peel with a potato peeler. Thinly slice beetroots. In a small bowl stir together jelly and lemon juice.

Cut an 18-inch (45cm) square of *heavy* silver foil (*see* photo 1, page 94). Place beetroots in the centre of the foil. Dot with butter or margarine. Fold up foil around beetroots; pour jelly mixture over beetroots (*see* photo 2, page 95).

Bring up 2 opposite edges of foil and, leaving space for expansion of steam, seal tightly (*see* photo 3, page 95). Tightly seal each end also.

Place foil packet on barbecue directly over *medium* coals (*see* photo 4, page 95). Cook 20 minutes. Turn packet over and cook 15 to 20 minutes more or until crisp-tender. Serve beetroots in individual bowls. Makes 2 or 3 servings.

Pan-Fried Vegetables

Planning to throw a party? Looking for something hot to really make it sizzle? Dazzle your guests with delicately pan-fried okra bites or cucumber chips.

Each vegetable is dipped in a light coating and then fried to a golden brown. The coating helps retain moistness, so they simply melt in your mouth.

You'll be the hit of the party and the talk of the town with these delicious little vegetable appetisers.

Fried Okra

Fried Okra

½ **pound (225g) okra**
2 **eggs**
   Several dashes bottled hot pepper
      sauce
2 **ounces (50g) cornmeal**
1¼ **ounces (30g) fine dry seasoned bread**
      crumbs
2 **fluid ounces (55ml) cooking oil**
   Taco sauce (optional)

Wash okra, cut off stems, and cut into ½-inch-thick (1cm) slices. In a small bowl beat together eggs and hot pepper sauce. In another small bowl combine cornmeal and bread crumbs.

Stir okra slices in egg mixture to coat; drain off excess egg mixture. Then toss okra slices in cornmeal mixture (see photo 1).

In a large frying pan heat cooking oil (see photo 2). Carefully add *half* of the okra to hot oil (see photo 3). Cook over medium-high heat for 2 to 3 minutes on each side or until brown (see photo 4). Drain well on kitchen papers. Repeat with remaining okra, adding oil if necessary. Serve okra warm with taco sauce, if desired. Serves 4.

2 Pour cooking oil into frying pan and heat over medium-high heat. Watch closely—it takes only 1 to 2 minutes to heat this small amount of oil.

3 Lower the okra slices *gently* into the hot oil with a large slotted spatula or slotted spoon. Dropping the food into the frying pan can splash the hot oil on your hand and arm.

1 Dip the okra slices in the beaten egg and then toss in the cornmeal mixture, as shown. Using a fork makes quick work of this and keeps your fingers clean.

4 Turn the okra slices over when the first side is golden brown. It takes 2 to 3 minutes for each side to brown.

Fried Cucumber Chips

Dunk crispy cucumber chips in either a snappy mustard sauce or a cool dill dip.

2 **medium cucumbers**
1 **beaten egg**
2 **ounces (50g) natural yogurt**
2 **tablespoons milk**
6 **ounces (175g) finely crushed whole wheat crackers *or* grated wheat wafers**
3 **fluid ounces (80ml) cooking oil**
   Soured-Cream-Dill Dip *or*
   Mustard Sauce (optional)

Peel cucumbers, if desired. Cut into ¼-inch (.5cm) slices. In a small bowl beat egg; stir in yogurt and milk.

Dip cucumber slices into egg mixture; drain off excess egg mixture. Coat cucumber slices with finely crushed crackers or wheat wafers (see photo 1).

In a large frying pan heat cooking oil (see photo 2). Carefully add *half* of the cucumber slices to hot oil (see photo 3). Cook over medium-high heat for 1 to 2 minutes on each side or until golden brown (see photo 4). Drain well on kitchen papers. Repeat with remaining slices, adding more oil if necessary. Serve warm with Soured-Cream-Dill Dip or Mustard Sauce, if desired. Makes 4 to 6 servings.

Soured-Cream-Dill Dip: Combine 4 ounces (110g) *soured cream,* 1 tablespoon thinly sliced *spring onion,* ¼ teaspoon finely grated *lemon peel,* ¼ teaspoon *Worcestershire sauce,* and ⅛ teaspoon dried *dill.* Stir in *milk,* if necessary, to make of dipping consistency (about 1 to 2 teaspoons). Cover and chill.

Mustard Sauce: In a small bowl combine 2 ounces (50g) *natural yogurt,* 2 ounces (50g) *soured cream,* and 1 tablespoon *French mustard.* Cover and chill.

Delectable Deep-Fried Vegetables

We, the jury, find these crisp tidbits responsible for a heavenly aroma, delicious taste, and a scrumptious flavour.

As evidence, we submit an assortment of fried vegetables, including the ever-popular Chips and Cheesy Beer-Batter Onion Rings plus exciting Oriental Vegetable Tempura.

We think your verdict will be unanimous—and that you'll find yourself returning to the scene for more!

Cheesy Beer-Batter Onion Rings

Cheesy Beer-Batter Onion Rings

- **1** slightly beaten egg
- **4** ounces (110g) plain flour
- **6** fluid ounces (165ml) beer
- **1** ounce (25g) grated Parmesan cheese
- **1** tablespoon cooking oil
- **3** medium (450g) Spanish onions, sliced ¼ inch (.5cm) thick (about 1 pound [450g])

  Cooking oil *or* lard for deep-fat frying

For batter, in a small bowl combine egg, flour, beer, cheese, and 1 tablespoon oil. Stir just until moistened. Separate onions into rings; pat dry with kitchen papers to prevent spattering.

In a heavy, deep 96-fluid-ounce (2.7l) saucepan or deep-fat fryer heat cooking oil or lard to 375°F (190°C) (see photo 1). Dip onion rings into batter; drain off excess batter (see photo 2). Carefully add 4 or 5 onion rings at a time to deep hot oil (see photo 3, page 100). Fry for 1 to 2 minutes or until golden brown, turning once (see photo 3, opposite).

Remove rings from hot oil. Drain on kitchen papers (see photo 4). Sprinkle with salt, if desired. Keep fried rings in a 300°F (150°C) gas mark 2 oven while frying remaining rings. Serves 6 to 8.

2 Use a long-handled fork to lift the onion rings out of the batter. Hold each onion ring above the bowl for a few seconds. This allows the excess batter to drip away.

1 Add enough cooking oil or lard to fill the pan about ⅓ to ½ full. Use a deep-fat frying thermometer to help you monitor the temperature. Be sure the bulb doesn't touch the pan.

3 Use the long-handled fork to turn the onion rings over when they are golden brown on the first side, as shown.

4 Transfer the fried onion rings to a baking tin lined with several layers of kitchen papers and spread them out to drain thoroughly.

Oriental Vegetable Tempura

½ **pound (225g) French beans**
½ **pound (225g) courgette**
½ **pound (225g) fresh mushrooms**
½ **pound (225g) broccoli florets**
 Sweet and Sour Sauce
5 **ounces (150g) plain flour**
2 **tablespoons cornflour**
¼ **teaspoon salt**
1 **beaten egg yolk**
8 **fluid ounces (220ml) ice cold water**
2 **egg whites**
 Cooking oil *or* lard for deep-fat frying

Cut French beans into 2-inch (5cm) pieces. Cut courgette into ¼-inch (.5cm) slices; cut slices in half or quarters if large. Cut large mushrooms in half. Pat beans, courgette, mushrooms, and broccoli dry with kitchen papers. Set aside. Prepare Sweet and Sour Sauce. Set aside.

For batter, in a medium bowl stir together flour, cornflour, and salt. Make a well in the centre. Combine egg yolk and ice cold water; add all at once to flour mixture. Stir just until moistened.

In a small mixer bowl beat egg whites with an electric mixer on medium speed or with a rotary beater until stiff peaks form (tips stand straight) (see photo 2, page 114). Gently fold beaten egg whites into batter. Do not allow batter to stand more than a few minutes before using.

In a heavy, deep 96-fluid-ounce (2.7l) saucepan or deep-fat fryer heat cooking oil or lard to 375°F (190°C) (see photo 1, page 104). Using a long-handled fork, dip vegetables into batter; drain off excess batter (see photo 2, page 104). Carefully add a few vegetables at a time to hot oil (see photo 3, page 100). Fry 2 to 3 minutes or until golden brown, turning once (see photo 3, page 105).

With a slotted spoon carefully remove vegetables from oil. Drain on kitchen papers (see photo 4, page 105). Keep fried vegetables hot in a 300°F (150°C) gas mark 2 oven while frying remaining vegetables. Serve with Sweet and Sour Sauce. Makes 8 servings.

Sweet and Sour Sauce: In a small saucepan combine 2 ounces (50g) *soft brown sugar* and 1 tablespoon *cornflour.* Stir in 3 fluid ounces (80ml) *chicken broth,* 3 fluid ounces (80ml) *red wine vinegar,* 1 tablespoon *soy sauce,* 1 teaspoon grated *root ginger,* and 2 cloves *garlic,* minced. Cook and stir until thickened and bubbly. Cook and stir 2 minutes more. Serve warm or cool. Makes about 1 cup.

Calico Fritters

8 **ounces (225g) packaged scone mix**
3 **ounces (75g) chopped fresh mushrooms**
2 **tablespoons sliced spring onion**
1 **tablespoon chopped pimento**
¼ **teaspoon celery seed**
1 **beaten egg yolk**
2 **ounces (50g) soured cream**
1 **egg white**
 Cooking oil *or* lard for deep-fat frying

In a medium bowl combine scone mix, mushrooms, onion, pimento, and celery seed. In a small bowl stir together egg yolk and soured cream; stir into mushroom mixture just until moistened. Set aside.

In a small mixer bowl beat egg white with a rotary beater until stiff peaks form (tips stand straight) (see photo 2, page 114). Gently fold beaten egg white into mushroom mixture.

In a heavy, deep 96-fluid-ounce (2.7l) saucepan or deep-fat fryer heat cooking oil or lard to 375°F (190°C) (see photo 1, page 104). Carefully add a few fritters at a time to hot oil by pushing mushroom mixture from a tablespoon into hot oil (see photo 3, page 100). Fry for 1 to 2 minutes or until golden brown, turning once (see photo 3, page 105).

Using a slotted spoon remove fritters from oil. Drain on kitchen papers (see photo 4, page 105). Keep hot in a 300°F (180°C) gas mark 2 oven while frying remaining fritters. Serves 6.

Chips

A special treat—homemade chips, shoestring potatoes, or potato crisps.

**4   medium baking potatoes
     Cooking oil *or* lard for deep-fat frying**

Peel potatoes. To prevent darkening, immerse peeled potatoes in a bowl of cold water until ready to cut. Cut potatoes lengthwise into ⅜-inch (.75cm) strips using a knife, chip cutter, or crinkle cutter. Return potato strips to bowl of cold water until ready to fry.

In a heavy, deep 96-fluid-ounce (2.7l) saucepan or deep-fat fryer heat cooking oil or lard to 375°F (190°C) (see photo 1, page 104). *Thoroughly* pat pototoes dry with kitchen towels to prevent splattering. Carefully add a few potatoes at a time to hot oil (see photo 3, page 100). Fry 6 to 7 minutes or until crisp and golden brown, turning once (see photo 3, page 105).

With a slotted spoon carefully remove potatoes from hot oil. Drain on kitchen towels (see photo 4, page 105). Sprinkle with salt, if desired. Keep chips hot in a 300°F (150°C) gas mark 2 oven while frying remaining potatoes. Makes 4 to 6 servings.

Shoestring Potatoes: Peel potatoes; immerse in a bowl of cold water until ready to cut. Using sharp knife, cut potatoes into thin julienne strips (see photo 3, page 9). Return potatoes to bowl of cold water until ready to fry. Continue as above, *except* fry a small amount of potatoes 3 to 4 minutes.

Potato Crisps: Peel potatoes. Immerse peeled potatoes in a bowl of cold water until ready to cut. Using a food processor or rotary processor, slice potatoes into thin slices. *(Or,* for very thin crisps, use a potato peeler to slice potatoes.) Return potatoes to bowl of cold water until ready to fry. Continue as directed above, *except* fry a small amount of thin potatoes for 4 to 5 minutes. *(Or,* fry a small amount of very thin potatoes 3 to 4 minutes).

Fried Asparagus

When fresh asparagus is at its seasonal best, serve this cheesy appetiser to a gathering of friends.

**1   slightly beaten egg
6   fluid ounces (165ml) milk
2½   ounces (60g) plain flour
2   ounces (50g) cornmeal
¾   ounce (15g) Italian dry salad dressing
       mix
1   pound (450g) asparagus
     Cooking oil *or* lard for deep-fat frying
     Grated Parmesan cheese**

For batter, in a medium bowl stir together egg and milk. Stir in flour, cornmeal, and dry salad dressing mix; stir until well mixed. Set aside.

Wash asparagus and scrape off scales, if desired. Break off bases at point where spears snap easily; discard bases. Cut large asparagus in half lengthwise. Cut asparagus in half crosswise. Thoroughly pat dry with kitchen papers.

In a heavy, deep 96-fluid-ounce (2.7l) saucepan or deep-fat fryer heat cooking oil or lard to 375°F (190°C) (see photo 1, page 104). Using a long-handled fork dip asparagus into batter; drain off excess batter (see photo 2, page 104). Carefully add 4 or 5 asparagus spears at a time to hot oil (see photo 3, page 100). Fry for 1 to 2 minutes or until golden brown, turning once (see photo 3, page 105).

With a slotted spoon carefully remove asparagus from hot oil. Drain on kitchen papers (see photo 4, page 105). Roll asparagus in Parmesan cheese. Keep fried asparagus hot in a 300°F (150°C) gas mark 2 oven while frying remaining asparagus. Makes 12 servings.

Whole-in-One Pizza

Get your dinner in full swing with this deep-dish vegetable pizza.

Tee up this recipe with thick, rich sieved tomatoes, followed by a snappy sauerkraut topping. Finish out the round with lots of gooey melted cheese with caraway seed.

For a pizza that's right on par with any vegetable lover, sink your teeth into this one-dish delight.

German-Style Deep-Dish Pizza

German-Style Deep-Dish Pizza

- 6   **ounces (175g) plain flour**
- 1   **packet active dried yeast**
- ½   **teaspoon caraway seed**
- 6   **fluid ounces (165ml) warm water (115°F [46°C] to 120°F [49°C])**
- 1   **tablespoon cooking oil**
- 3½   **ounces (85g) rye flour**
- 4   **ounces (110g) chopped onion**
- 1   **small green pepper, chopped**
- 1   **clove garlic, minced**
- 2   **tablespoons olive oil *or* cooking oil**
- 10½   **ounces (285g) tomatoes, peeled, seeded, and chopped (2 large), *or* 1 pound (450g) tinned tomatoes, drained and chopped**
- 6   **ounces (175g) tinned tomato puree**
- 1   **teaspoon dried basil, crushed**
- 1   **teaspoon dried oregano, crushed**
- 12   **ounces (350g) grated cheddar cheese**
- ¼   **teaspoon caraway seed**
- 16   **ounces (450g) tinned sauerkraut, rinsed, well drained, and snipped**
- 4   **ounces (110g) grated Parmesan cheese**

For crust, in a small mixer bowl combine plain flour, yeast, caraway seed, and ¾ teaspoon *salt*. Stir in water and 1 tablespoon oil. Beat with an electric mixer on low speed for 30 seconds, scraping bowl constantly. Beat on high speed for 3 minutes. Using a spoon, stir in about 2½ ounces (60g) of rye flour.

Turn dough out onto a lightly floured surface. Knead in enough remaining rye flour to make a moderately stiff dough that is smooth and elastic (6 to 8 minutes total) (see photo 1). Cover dough; let rest 10 minutes.

Grease a 14-inch (35cm) deep-dish pizza pan. On a lightly floured surface, roll dough into a 16-inch (40cm) circle (see photo 2). Wrap dough around rolling pin; unroll into the greased pan, extending dough 1 inch (2.5cm) up the sides of the pan. (*Or*, if using a 15x10x1-inch [37.5x25.5x2.5cm]) baking tin, grease tin. On a lightly floured surface, roll dough into a 16x11-inch [40x28cm] rectangle. Wrap dough around rolling pin; unroll into the greased pan,

extending dough ½ inch [1cm] up sides of the pan.) Cover and let rise until nearly double (30 to 45 minutes). Bake the 14-inch (35cm) crust in a 375°F (190°C) gas mark 5 oven for 15 to 18 minutes or until light brown. (*Or*, bake a 15x10-inch [37.5x25.5cm] crust about 12 minutes or until light brown.)

In a saucepan cook onion, green pepper, and garlic in 2 tablespoons hot olive oil or cooking oil until onion is tender. Stir in tomatoes, tomato puree, basil, and oregano. Bring to boiling; reduce heat. Simmer, covered, for 5 minutes.

Toss together cheese and caraway seed; sprinkle 4 ounces (110g) of mixture over crust (see photo 3). Spread tomato mixture over crust (see photo 4). Top with sauerkraut, remaining cheese mixture, and Parmesan cheese.

Bake the 14-inch (35cm) pizza about 20 minutes more or until bubbly. (*Or*, bake a 15x10-inch [37.5x25.5cm] pizza about 15 minutes.) Makes 6 main-dish servings.

1 Knead dough by pulling the ball of dough toward you with curved fingers. Then push down and away with the heel of your hand, as shown. Turn the dough, fold it over, and repeat the process.

2 Starting at the centre, roll the dough from the centre to the edge. Continue rolling from the centre to the edge, moving around in a circle until you have a 16-inch (40cm) circle of dough.

3 Evenly sprinkle 4 ounces (110g) of the cheese directly on the warm crust. This layer of cheese helps hold the pizza slices together for easy eating.

4 Gently spread the tomato mixture over the crust and first layer of cheese. Be sure to spread the mixture all the way to the edge.

So-Light Soufflés

Lights! Camera! Action! When you serve one of these showy soufflés as the star attraction, you can expect rave reviews.

The delicate flavour of vegetables co-stars with the light, airy texture of eggs, producing succulent soufflés that will play the lead in any meal.

Each a glamourous vegetable dish, these are soufflés you'll find worthy of a repeat performance.

Carrot Soufflé

Carrot Soufflé

4 eggs
6 ounces (175g) diced carrots *or* frozen sliced carrots
2 ounces (50g) chopped onion
2 ounces (50g) butter *or* margarine
1⅓ ounces (33g) plain flour
¼ teaspoon ground nutmeg
6 fluid ounces (165ml) milk
2 fluid ounces (55ml) dry white wine

Separate eggs (see photo 1). Set aside. In a small saucepan cook diced carrots and onions, covered, in a small amount of boiling water for 12 to 15 minutes or until tender. (*Or,* cook frozen carrots according to packet directions, *except* add onion). Drain well.

In a food-processor bowl or blender container place carrots and onion. Cover; process or blend until smooth (see photo 1, page 74).

In small saucepan melt butter or margarine. Stir in flour, nutmeg, and ¼ teaspoon *salt.* Add milk all at once. Cook and stir until thickened and bubbly. Remove from heat. Stir wine into sauce.

Add egg yolks to sauce; mix until well blended. Then add carrot mixture; mix well.

Beat egg whites until stiff peaks form (see photo 2). Gradually pour carrot mixture over beaten egg whites; fold to blend. Pour into an ungreased 64-fluid-ounce (1.8l) soufflé dish. Bake in a 350°F (180°C) gas mark 4 oven for 45 to 50 minutes or until a knife inserted near the centre comes out clean (see photo 3). Serve immediately. Makes 4 main-dish servings.

1 Slip the egg yolk back and forth from one shell half to the other so the egg white drains into a cup. If you get even a trace of yolk in the white, set it aside for scrambled eggs.

2 Beat the egg whites until they stand straight in stiff peaks when the beaters are lifted out, as shown. Allow about 1½ minutes to beat 4 egg whites with an electric mixer.

3 To see if the soufflé is ready, insert knife and move it slightly from side to side to enlarge the hole in the crust. Then the crust won't clean the knife as the knife is removed.

Courgette Soufflé

4	eggs
32	ounces (900g) grated courgette
2	ounces (50g) butter *or* margarine
1¼	ounces (30g) plain flour
1	teaspoon dried basil, crushed
¼	teaspoon salt
⅛	teaspoon ground red pepper
6	fluid ounces (165ml) milk
4	ounces (110g) grated cheddar cheese

Separate eggs (see photo 1). Set aside. Attach a collar to a 64-fluid-ounce (1.8l) soufflé dish by measuring enough silver foil to go around the dish plus 6 inches (15cm). Fold the foil into thirds lengthwise and lightly butter one side. With buttered side in, position the foil around the dish so the foil extends 2 inches (5cm) above the dish. Fold the ends of the foil until it is fastened securely. Set the dish aside.

In a small saucepan cook courgette, covered, in a small amount of boiling water about 5 minutes or until tender. Drain well, squeezing out liquid.

In saucepan melt butter or margarine. Stir in flour, basil, salt, and red pepper. Add milk all at once. Cook and stir until thickened and bubbly. Remove from heat. Stir in cheese until melted; stir in courgette. Add egg yolks; mix well.

Beat egg whites until stiff peaks form (see photo 2). Gradually pour courgette mixture over beaten whites; fold to blend. Pour into the prepared ungreased soufflé dish. Bake in a 350°F (180°C) gas mark 4 oven about 40 minutes or until a knife inserted near the centre comes out clean (see photo 3). Remove collar. Serve immediately. Makes 4 main-dish servings.

Cooking Fresh Vegetables

- Timings for this chart are approximate, so use them only as a guide to cook vegetables to desired tenderness.
- The maturity of a vegetable and the preparation method (whole, diced) cause some variation in timings. Cutting the vegetables into uniform pieces (for instance, halving large brussels sprouts) helps them cook more evenly.
- Except in stir-fry and microwave cooking, the amount of vegetables does not change the cooking time. For example, it takes the same amount of time to boil or steam ½ pound (225g) of asparagus as it does 1 pound (450g). In stir-frying and microwave cooking, the cooking time depends on the amount of the vegetable (see Beans for examples).
- All timings are for the crisp-tender stage, except for those vegetables that are eaten at a tender stage. For example, potatoes and mushrooms would be tender, not crisp-tender. Other vegetables may be cooked longer to desired tenderness.

ARTICHOKES

Boil: In a large amount of water for 20 to 25 minutes.
Steam: 25 minutes.
Microwave: One, 5 to 7 minutes; two, 7 to 10 minutes.

ASPARAGUS

Boil: Spears, 10 to 12 minutes; 1-inch (2.5cm) cuts, 7 minutes.
Steam: Spears, 8 to 10 minutes; 1-inch (2.5cm) cuts, 7 minutes.
Stir-fry: 1-inch (2.5cm) sliced pieces (¾ pound [350g] before trimming), 4 to 5 minutes.
Microwave: Spears (1 pound [450g]) before trimming), 7 to 9 minutes; 1-inch (2.5cm) cuts (12 ounces [350g]), 4 to 6 minutes; 1-inch (2.5cm) cuts (24 ounces [700g]), 6 to 8 minutes.

AUBERGINE

Boil: ¾-inch (2cm) cubes, 5 to 7 minutes.
Steam: ¾-inch (2cm) cubes, 8 minutes.

COOKING GUIDELINES

Boil: Add vegetables to saucepan with a small amount of lightly salted boiling water (about 4 fluid ounces ([110ml]). Return to boiling; reduce heat. Simmer, covered, until done.
Steam: Place steamer basket in saucepan. Add water to just below bottom of steamer basket. Bring to boiling. Add vegetables. Steam, covered, until done.
Grill: Arrange vegetables on the unheated rack of a grill pan. Grill 3 to 4 inches (7.5 to 10cm) from the heat, turning once, until done.
Stir-fry: Add 1 to 2 tablespoons cooking oil to a hot wok or large frying pan. Add vegetables (up to 1½ pounds [700 grams]) at a time) and stir-fry until done.
Microwave: Place vegetables in a microwave-safe casserole with 2 tablespoons water (except when noted). Micro-cook, covered, on 100% power (HIGH) until done.

Grill: 1-inch (2.5cm) slices, 10 to 12 minutes.
Stir-fry: ¾-inch (2cm) cubes (27 ounces [785g]), 6 to 7 minutes.
Microwave: ¾-inch (2cm) cubes (30 ounces [850g]) 4 to 6 minutes.

BEANS, Dry

Boil: After soaking: butter bean, 45 to 60 minutes; haricot, 75 to 90 minutes.

BEANS, French

Boil: 1-inch (2.5cm) pieces, 20 to 25 minutes;
Steam: 1-inch (2.5cm) pieces, 25 to 30 minutes.
Stir-fry: After precooking 4 minutes: 1-inch (2.5cm) pieces (½ pound [225g]), 3 minutes.
Microwave: 1-inch (2.5cm) pieces (½ pound [225g]), 10 to 12 minutes; 1-inch (2.5cm) pieces (1 pound [450g]), 16 to 19 minutes.

BEANS, Butter

Boil: 20 to 25 minutes.
Steam: 20 to 25 minutes.

BEETROOTS

Boil: Whole (not peeled), 35 to 50 minutes; slices or cubes, 20 minutes.
Microwave: Quarters (peeled) (1 pound [450g]), 12 to 14 minutes; slices or cubes (1 pound [450g]), 10 to 12 minutes.

BROCCOLI

Boil: Spears, 11 to 12 minutes; ½-inch (1cm) cuts, 10 to 12 minutes.
Steam: Spears, 12 to 14 minutes; ½-inch (1cm) cuts, 10 to 12 minutes.
Stir-fry: ½-inch (1cm) cuts (½ pound [225g]), 3 to 4 minutes.
Microwave: Spears (1 pound [450g]), 6 to 9 minutes; ½-inch (1cm) cuts (1 pound [450g]), 6 to 8 minutes.

BRUSSELS SPROUTS

Boil: 13 to 15 minutes.
Steam: 15 minutes.
Stir-fry: After precooking 5 minutes: whole or halves (½ pound [225g]), 5 minutes.
Microwave: Whole or halves (1 pound [450g]), 6 to 8 minutes; (½ pound [225g]), 3 to 5 minutes.

CABBAGE

Boil: Wedges, 10 to 12 minutes; grated, 5 to 7 minutes.
Steam: Wedges, 10 to 13 minutes; grated, 5 to 7 minutes.
Stir-fry: Grated (½ pound [225g]), 3 minutes.
Microwave: Six wedges, 10 to 12 minutes; grated (1 pound [450g]), 10 to 12 minutes.

CARROTS

Boil: Whole or strips, 15 to 20 minutes; slices, 12 to 14 minutes; grated, 5 minutes.
Steam: Slices, 15 minutes; diced, 12 to 15 minutes.
Stir-fry: Thin slices or julienne strips (6 ounces [175g]), 4 to 5 minutes.
Microwave: Slices (½ pound [225g]), 8 to 11 minutes.

CAULIFLOWER

Boil: Whole head, 12 to 15 minutes; florets, 7 to 10 minutes.
Steam: Whole head, 15 to 17 minutes; florets, 8 to 10 minutes.
Stir-fry: Thin slices (1 pound [450g]), 5 minutes.
Microwave: Whole head (1 to 1½ pounds [450 to 675g] after trimming; add 2 fluid ounces (55ml water), 8 to 10 minutes; florets (9 ounces [250g]), 4 to 6 minutes.

CELERIAC

Boil: Cubes, 10 minutes.
Steam: Cubes, 10 minutes.
Stir-fry: Cubes or strips (½ pound [225g]), 3 to 5 minutes.
Microwave: Cubes (7 ounces [200g]), 4 to 5 minutes.

CELERY

Boil: Slices, 7 minutes.
Steam: Slices, 7 minutes.
Stir-fry: Thin slices (½ pound ([25g]), 3 to 4 minutes.
Microwave: ½-inch (1cm) slices (4 ounces [110g]), 3 to 5 minutes; chopped (5 ounces [150g]), 3 to 5 minutes.

CHAYOTE

Boil: ¾-inch (2cm) cubes, 5 minutes.
Steam: ¾-inch (2cm) cubes, 8 minutes.
Microwave: ¾-inch (2cm) cubes (1 medium), 4 to 6 minutes.

DAIKON

Boil: Strips, 5 minutes.
Steam: Strips, 5 to 7 minutes.
Stir-fry: Strips (½ pound [225g]), 2½ minutes
Microwave: Strips (½ pound [225g]), 3 to 4 minutes.

Cooking Fresh Vegetables *(continued)*

GREENS

Boil: Torn, 9 to 12 minutes.
Steam: Torn, 10 to 12 minutes.
Stir-fry: Torn (½ pound [225g]), 1 to 2 minutes.
Microwave: Torn (24 ounces [700g]), 7 to 9 minutes.

JERUSALEM ARTICHOKE

Boil: Slices (6 to 8 fluid ounces [165 to 220ml] water), 8 to 10 minutes.
Steam: ¼-inch (.5cm) slices, 10 to 12 minutes.
Microwave: Slices (1 pound [450g]), 5 to 7 minutes

JICAMA

Boil: Cubes, 15 minutes.
Steam: Cubes, 15 minutes.
Microwave: ½-inch (1cm) cubes (13 ounces [375g]), 6 to 8 minutes.

KOHL-RABI

Boil: ¾-inch (2cm) cubes, 8 minutes.
Steam: ¾-inch (2cm) cubes, 8 minutes.
Microwave: Cubes (1 pound [450g]), 4 to 6 minutes.

LEEKS

Boil: ½-inch (1cm) slices, 10 minutes.
Steam: ½-inch (1cm) slices, 10 minutes.
Stir-fry: ½-inch (1cm) slices (10 ounces [275g]), 3 to 4 minutes.
Microwave: ½-inch slices (10 ounces [275g]), 3 to 4 minutes.

MANGE TOUT

Boil: 2 to 4 minutes.
Steam: 2 to 4 minutes.
Stir-fry: ½ pound (225g), 2 to 3 minutes.
Microwave: ½ pound (225g), 3 to 5 minutes.

MUSHROOMS

Boil: Whole, 10 to 12 minutes.
Steam: Whole, 10 to 12 minutes.
Grill: Whole, 10 minutes.
Stir-fry: Slices (4½ ounces [125g]), 1 minute.
Microwave: Slices (9 ounces [250g]), 2½ to 3½ minutes.

OKRA

Boil: Slices, 8 minutes.
Steam: Slices, 5 to 7 minutes.
Microwave: Slices (½ pound [225g]), 3 to 5 minutes.

ONIONS

Boil: Quarters and small whole, 25 to 30 minutes; slices, 10 minutes.
Steam: Slices, 10 to 12 minutes.
Stir-fry: Chopped (1 medium), 2 minutes; thin wedges (1 medium), 3 minutes.
Microwave: Quarters (4 medium), 6 to 8 minutes; slices or chopped (1 medium), 2 to 3 minutes.

PARSNIPS

Boil: Cubes, 12 to 15 minutes.
Steam: ¼-inch (.5cm) slices and cubes, 12 to 15 minutes.
Stir-fry: Thin slices (6 ounces [175g]), 4 to 5 minutes.
Microwave: ¼-inch (½cm) slices (6 ounces [175g]), 4 to 6 minutes.

PEAS, Green

Boil: Shelled, 10 to 12 minutes.
Steam: Shelled, 12 to 15 minutes.
Microwave: Shelled (¾ pound [350g]), 6 to 8 minutes.

PEPPERS, Green, Sweet Red, and Yellow

Boil: 3 to 5 minutes.
Steam: 5 to 8 minutes.
Stir-Fry: ¾-inch (2cm) pieces (1 medium) (6 ounces [175g]), 1½ minutes.
Microwave: Chopped (1 medium) (6 ounces [175g]), 3 to 5 minutes.

POTATOES

Boil: Whole, 25 to 40 minutes; quarters, 20 to 25 minutes; tiny new, 13 to 15 minutes; diced, 12 minutes.
Steam: Quartered, 20 to 25 minutes; tiny new, 20 minutes; diced, 12 minutes.
Bake: Whole, 40 to 60 minutes at 425°F (220°C) gas mark 7; 70 to 80 minutes at 350°F (180°C) gas mark 4.
Microwave: Prick skin in several places. Whole, 1 medium, 5 to 7 minutes; 2 medium, 7 to 9 minutes; 4 medium, 13 to 16 minutes. Quarters (4 medium), 10 to 12 minutes. Cubes and slices (about 3 medium), 6 to 8. Tiny new potatoes (about 8), 6 to 8 minutes.

SPINACH

Boil: Torn, 3 to 5 minutes.
Steam: Torn, 4 minutes.
Stir-fry: Torn (½ pound [225g]), 1 to 2 minutes.
Microwave: Leaves (1½ pounds [700g]), 7 to 9 minutes.

SQUASH, Winter (Acorn, Butternut)

Boil: Slices, 10 minutes; cubes, 6 to 8 minutes.
Steam: Quarters, 25 to 30 minutes; slices, 7 to 8 minutes; cubes 6 to 8 minutes.
Bake: Halves, 30 minutes at 350°F (180°C) gas mark 4, cut side down, then for 10 to 20 minutes cut side up.
Microwave: Acorn squash halves (2), 6½ to 8½ minutes; butternut squash halves (2), 10 to 13 minutes.

SQUASH, Summer (Courgette, Yellow)

Boil: Slices, 5 to 10 minutes.
Steam: Slices, 5 to 10 minutes.

Stir-fry: ¼-inch (.5cm) slices (1 medium squash), 3 to 3½ minutes.
Microwave: ¼-inch (.5cm) slices (1 pound [450g]), 6 to 8 minutes.

SWEET CORN

Boil: On the cob, 6 to 8 minutes; kernels, 4 minutes.
Steam: On the cob, 6 to 8 minutes; kernels, 4 to 5 minutes.
Microwave: On the cob, 1 ear, 2 to 3 minutes; 2 ears, 4 to 5 minutes; 3 ears, 6 to 7 minutes; 4 ears, 8 to 9 minutes; 5 ears, 10 to 12 minutes; 6 ears, 12 to 14 minutes.
Kernels (¾ pound [350g]), 5 to 6 minutes.

SWEET POTATOES

Boil: Whole, 25 to 35 minutes; ¼-inch (.5cm) slices, 15 minutes.
Steam: Quarters, 12 minutes; ¼-inch (.5cm) slices, 15 minutes.
Bake: Whole, 40 to 45 minutes at 375°F (190°C) gas mark 5.
Stir-fry: ¼-inch (.5cm) slices (10 ounces [275g]), 4 to 5 minutes.
Microwave: Prick skin in several places. Whole, 4 medium (about 1 pound [450g]), 7 to 9 minutes. Cubes, (3 medium (about 1 pound [450g]), 6 to 8 minutes.

TOMATOES

Boil: Slices and cubes, 10 to 12 minutes.
Grill: ½-inch (1cm) slices, 3 to 4 minutes.
Stir-fry: 1 minute to heat through.
Microwave: ¼-inch (.5cm) slices (4 medium), 3 to 5 minutes.

TURNIPS

Boil: ½-inch (1cm) cubes and ¼-inch (.5cm) slices, 10 to 15 minutes.
Steam: Cubes, 20 to 25 minutes.
Stir-fry: ½-inch (1cm) cubes (10 ounces [275g]), 3½ to 4½ minutes.
Microwave: ½-inch (1cm) cubes (13 ounces [375g]), 10 to 12 minutes.

Kohl-Rabi

Leek

Jicama

Okra

Unusual Vegetables

Supermarket produce sections look like works of art with the beautiful array of fresh vegetables now available. And, no doubt, some of these vegetables will be new to you.

This guide acquaints you with a few of these unusual vegetables. It lets you select and prepare each like an expert. Check the index for recipes using these vegetables.

Kohl-Rabi

It may look like a bulb, but kohl-rabi is actually a stem vegetable that has the flavours of cabbage and turnips combined. It can be green, lavender, or white in colour.

Choose small kohl-rabi, about the size of a tennis ball or smaller, for a mild flavour and crisp texture.

To use kohl-rabi, cut off any leaves or stalk and rinse. Peel it before or after cooking. Or, peel it to use raw in salads and on relish trays as you would celery or turnips. The leaves of kohl-rabi also can be cooked like spinach.

Leek

Leeks look like a gigantic spring onion but have a milder, sweeter flavour than onions. When selecting them, choose leeks with a long white base, not those that have a bulb like spring onions. Choose small to medium-size leeks with fresh green leaves.

Wait until you're ready to use the leeks to wash them. Cut off the roots and tough outer leaves. Split the leek in half lengthwise and swish it in water. Then rinse it thoroughly under running water to remove all the sand.

Use leeks as you would onions—either raw or cooked until crisp-tender. Leeks also make attractive garnishes.

Daikon

Chayote

*Jerusalem
Artichoke*

Jicama
Jicama (HEE kuh muh), a root vegetable, is a staple in Mexico. It's crisp with a mild, sweet flavour.

Purchase a firm jicama with no mold. Store in a cool, dark place or in the refrigerator. When you're ready to use the jicama, peel off the skin and fibrous outer layer with a knife. Slice or dice to use raw in salads and on relish trays. Or, try cooking jicamas as you would cook potatoes.

Okra
These small green pods are a favourite of cooks in the southern part of the United States. Their natural thickening is a must in classic Cajun gumbo. Favourite ways of using okra include batter-frying, pickling, and stewing with tomatoes.

Choose small, crisp okra, and avoid large, woody ones or any that are turning black. Use the okra within a few days or freeze it for extended storage.

Daikon
Daikon (DIKE un) is a long, white Japanese radish sometimes called mooli or muli. It's common in Oriental cookery—in stir-frys, as pickles (Takuan), or with raw fish. Daikon's peppery flavour is similar to a hot radish.

Choose firm, smooth daikon with no cracks or wilted leaves. Cut off any leaves and store it in the refrigerator for a few days. Peel it with a vegetable peeler and grate or slice it. Daikon is served raw as a relish, cooked like turnips in soups, or stir-fried.

Chayote
Chayote (chah YOTE ee), a pear-shaped squash, is also called mirliton or mango squash. It tastes like apples and cucumbers and its texture is similar to cucumbers. It is most common in the southern United States and Mexico.

When purchasing chayote, look for small, firm, unblemished ones. They can be boiled, baked, or steamed, either peeled or unpeeled. Chayote can be substituted for squash in salads, soups, and desserts.

Jerusalem Artichoke
A native of North America and no relation to the familiar globe artichoke, these small tubers are also called sunchokes. When eaten raw, they have a sweet, nutty flavor and crunchy texture. When Jerusalem artichokes are cooked, their flavour is similar to globe artichokes.

Use Jerusalem artichokes raw in salads and with dips. Or, cook them like potatoes. Leave the peel on to cook and then peel, if desired.

Nutrition Analysis Chart

Use these analyses to compare nutritional values of different recipes. This information was calculated using Agriculture Handbook Number 8, published by the United States Department of Agriculture, as the primary source. Figures are based on the ingredients used in the American version of each recipe.

In compiling the nutrition analyses, we made the following assumptions:

● For main-dish recipes containing meat, the nutrition analyses were calculated using measurements for cooked meat.

● Garnishes and optional ingredients were not included in the nutrition analyses.

● If a marinade was brushed over a food during cooking, the analysis includes all of the marinade.

● When two ingredient options appear in a recipe, calculations were made using the first one.

● For ingredients of variable weight (such as "2½- to 3-pound [1kg125g to 1kg350g] chicken") or for recipes with a serving range ("Makes 4 to 6 servings"), calculations were made using the first figure.

	Per Serving						U.S. Recommended Daily Allowances Per Serving (%)							
	Calories	Protein (g)	Carbohydrate (g)	Fat (g)	Sodium (mg)	Potassium (mg)	Protein	Vitamin A	Vitamin C	Thiamine	Riboflavin	Niacin	Calcium	Iron
Appetisers														
Appetising Antipasto (p. 8)	196	10	8	15	554	399	15	155	80	7	11	7	19	8
Artichokes with Citrus Butter (p. 58)	260	3	13	23	309	356	4	21	23	5	3	4	5	9
Cucumber-Spinach Dip with Crudités (p. 11)	15	0	1	1	30	30	1	2	1	0	1	0	2	0
Fried Asparagus (p. 107)	85	4	9	4	252	141	6	7	12	6	6	3	6	3
Fried Cucumber Chips (p. 101)	262	5	21	19	149	263	7	3	10	11	9	7	6	7
Soured-Cream-Dill Dip (p. 101)	66	1	2	6	20	50	2	5	1	1	3	0	4	0
Main Dishes														
Barbecue-Style Potatoes (p. 22)	660	23	92	23	1279	1236	35	14	63	17	20	36	29	75
Black Beans and Rice (p. 83)	379	24	64	3	763	789	37	0	11	58	13	23	11	31
Cantonese Beef with Hoisin Sauce (p. 91)	296	17	21	17	782	647	27	222	81	15	14	19	8	19
Carrot Soufflé (p. 114)	393	10	21	19	362	337	15	319	11	11	17	5	11	10
Cheesy Brussels Sprouts and Tofu (p. 68)	423	20	26	28	821	493	31	26	68	12	18	11	34	13
Cheesy Potato (p. 22)	489	17	79	13	270	1013	26	8	38	14	19	26	33	68
Courgette Soufflé (p. 115)	360	16	11	28	520	300	25	25	8	10	22	4	31	11
Crab- and Avocado-Stuffed Courgette (p. 51)	282	13	10	23	355	829	20	41	22	16	9	17	6	10
Cream Cheese Potato (p. 22)	646	15	81	30	446	1016	23	16	43	17	16	29	11	67
Curried Chicken in Potatoes (p. 23)	540	25	85	12	681	1202	38	5	67	18	17	59	9	74
Curried Sausage-Meat-Stuffed Squash (p. 48)	499	17	63	22	859	1319	27	18	36	58	11	34	13	20
Curried Vegetables (p. 88)	347	12	44	14	332	555	18	246	115	20	7	25	10	19
Garden Potato (p. 22)	514	22	81	12	442	1088	33	9	43	14	22	27	30	69
German-Style Deep-Dish Pizza (p. 110)	499	24	42	27	1427	609	38	38	56	23	33	18	55	21
Greek Potato (p. 22)	411	12	85	4	231	1182	18	3	41	16	21	27	22	69
Herbed Bean Stew (p. 82)	358	15	48	13	925	855	23	15	37	39	20	18	19	28
Low-Cal Potato (p. 22)	387	11	84	1	92	1161	18	1	39	16	21	27	20	67

	Per Serving					U.S. Recommended Daily Allowances Per Serving (%)							
	Calories	Protein (g)	Carbohydrate (g)	Fat (g)	Sodium (mg)	Potassium (mg)	Protein	Vitamin A	Vitamin C	Thiamine	Riboflavin	Niacin	Calcium	Iron

Main Dishes (continued)

	Calories	Protein (g)	Carbo. (g)	Fat (g)	Sodium (mg)	Potassium (mg)	Protein	Vit A	Vit C	Thiamine	Riboflavin	Niacin	Calcium	Iron
Meat and Potatoes (p. 22)	559	33	85	10	158	1319	51	0	27	20	23	49	7	86
Mexican Cheese Potatoes (p.22)	875	36	91	41	1340	1497	56	12	38	17	32	50	34	84
Pork and Pepper Stir-Fry (p. 91)	215	19	8	12	563	467	30	15	98	43	13	21	1	11
Potatoes with Prawn Creole Topper (p. 20)	425	19	87	1	290	1373	29	14	48	18	13	30	13	76
Prawn-Stuffed Artichokes (p. 16)	271	20	19	14	221	679	30	16	22	8	17	14	28	15
Savoury Stuffed Aubergine (p. 51)	317	26	27	12	782	834	40	122	48	21	20	22	33	20
Try-a-Topper Taters (p. 22)	508	10	82	17	78	1089	15	13	39	15	18	26	15	67

Salads

Creamy Chayote (p. 17)	90	5	8	5	64	245	7	4	10	4	6	9	8	3
Creamy Curry-Vegetable Salad (p. 10)	125	4	10	9	33	298	7	3	16	4	5	2	6	8
Crunchy Jicama Salad (p. 10)	211	3	15	16	206	121	5	4	33	3	4	0	5	8
Tomato-Mushroom Salad (p. 11)	84	1	5	7	8	265	2	30	30	5	7	5	2	5
Wilted Spinach Salad (p. 56)	105	8	12	4	278	1057	12	222	57	13	26	12	19	28

Side Dishes

Asparagus with Almond Sauce (p. 43)	89	3	5	7	79	278	5	14	24	6	8	5	4	4
Aubergine Pizzas (p. 32)	133	8	10	7	376	180	12	10	6	6	7	5	20	5
Barbecued Asparagus with Sorrel Dressing (p. 96)	135	5	6	11	94	406	7	26	45	9	10	7	6	5
Barbecued Beetroots (p. 97)	266	2	41	12	222	481	3	9	23	4	2	3	3	10
Beer-Cheese Broccoli and Onion (p. 70)	146	7	9	10	273	304	10	25	65	5	11	3	16	4
Broccoli with Brie Sauce (p. 44)	101	5	6	7	178	274	8	25	73	4	11	3	8	4
Calico Fritters (p. 106)	148	3	15	9	267	94	5	4	4	8	9	6	3	6
Cauliflower-Asparagus Stir-Fry (p. 86)	87	4	9	5	8	453	6	16	74	10	9	7	4	5
Cauliflower Supreme (p. 71)	167	5	10	13	277	299	7	24	57	6	8	3	11	5
Chayote-Rice Stir-Fry (p. 89)	172	6	25	6	306	347	9	8	39	12	9	11	8	10
Cheesy Beer-Batter Onion Rings (p. 104)	194	6	19	10	118	156	9	2	7	10	7	6	10	7
Cheesy Chokes and Leeks (p. 43)	128	5	19	4	91	425	8	5	12	12	8	6	15	17
Chips (p. 107)	198	3	27	9	9	815	5	0	34	9	3	11	1	6
Creamed Parsnips and Peas (p. 44)	149	5	21	6	163	360	7	11	23	13	9	7	8	7
Creamy Caraway Cabbage (p. 70)	220	5	15	16	120	460	8	14	42	9	19	10	15	7
Creole-Style Vegetables (p. 57)	46	2	10	0	113	370	3	25	48	11	3	5	7	6
Crumb-Capped French Beans (p. 16)	87	3	13	3	189	140	4	10	10	5	5	4	4	5
Curried Cauliflower Puree (p. 64)	18	2	4	0	11	269	2	0	63	4	2	2	2	3
Dilled French Beans and Tomatoes (p. 89)	87	2	6	7	46	182	3	14	14	4	6	3	5	4
Fried Okra (p. 100)	229	5	14	17	85	199	8	9	11	10	7	5	6	7
German-Style Stuffed Turnips (p. 50)	134	4	13	8	425	294	6	7	29	5	6	3	11	4
Glazed Onions (p. 16)	126	2	17	6	64	259	3	5	39	6	1	1	4	5
Grilled Tomatoes (p. 33)	63	2	5	4	113	156	4	20	16	3	3	3	6	4
Harvard Beetroots (p. 56)	86	2	15	3	169	357	2	2	13	3	1	2	2	6
Herbed Barbecued Potatoes (p. 97)	221	3	26	12	126	777	5	9	32	8	3	11	1	6
Honeyed Turnips and Apples (p. 57)	144	1	23	6	109	358	2	5	29	6	2	3	5	3
Kohl-Rabi Bake (p. 94)	102	5	5	7	292	281	7	7	48	3	4	2	11	2
Lemon-Basil Carrots (p. 45)	99	1	11	6	97	359	2	612	13	7	4	5	3	3
Lemony Pepper Corn on the Cob (p. 97)	159	3	18	10	102	264	5	12	8	12	3	8	1	4

	Per Serving						U.S. Recommended Daily Allowances Per Serving (%)						
	Calories	Protein (g)	Carbohydrate (g)	Fat (g)	Sodium (mg)	Potassium (mg)	Protein	Vitamin A	Vitamin C	Thiamine	Riboflavin	Niacin	Calcium	Iron

Side Dishes (continued)

	Calories	Protein (g)	Carbohydrate (g)	Fat (g)	Sodium (mg)	Potassium (mg)	Protein	Vitamin A	Vitamin C	Thiamine	Riboflavin	Niacin	Calcium	Iron
Mange Tout and Summer Squash (p.57)	79	2	7	6	95	172	3	8	27	6	4	3	4	4
Mashed Potatoes (p. 65)	141	3	21	6	106	624	4	4	37	7	3	8	1	5
Mexican Potatoes (p. 64)	136	3	23	4	160	667	5	7	52	8	5	9	5	5
New England Baked Beans (p. 82)	226	9	37	5	141	636	14	0	2	18	6	6	10	22
New Potatoes with Mustard Sauce (p. 45)	193	5	25	8	340	728	7	6	27	9	8	9	9	6
Orange Carrots and Sprouts (p. 17)	116	4	16	5	68	518	6	320	86	11	6	6	5	9
Oriental Beans (p. 96)	36	2	8	0	519	181	3	8	12	3	4	4	2	6
Oriental Turnips (p. 65)	91	1	9	6	222	245	2	4	28	3	2	3	4	3
Oriental Vegetable Tempura (p. 106)	160	5	19	8	90	330	8	10	45	10	15	10	2	10
Orzo- and Feta-Stuffed Pepper Shells (p. 50)	212	7	21	12	410	333	11	22	129	15	12	9	13	11
Potato Crisps (p. 107)	198	3	27	9	9	815	5	0	34	9	3	11	1	6
Sesame Broccoli (p. 14)	97	4	7	7	91	396	6	42	130	6	9	4	6	7
Shoestring Potatoes (p. 107)	198	3	27	9	9	815	5	0	34	9	3	11	1	6
Southern Sweet Potatoes (p. 62)	298	4	48	11	215	395	5	687	48	12	15	6	4	7
South-of-the-Border Taters (p. 23)	422	9	85	6	474	1085	14	9	63	15	12	27	7	68
Spaghetti Squash with Tomato-Dill Sauce (p. 54)	86	2	13	3	288	444	3	22	27	70	61	3	2	6
Sweet Corn Relish (p. 58)	47	1	12	0	47	75	1	2	7	1	1	2	1	1
Sweet 'n' Sour Vegetables (p. 88)	86	2	13	4	15	323	3	2	48	6	11	9	4	6
Sweet-Sour Cabbage (p. 40)	134	3	31	1	258	600	5	51	186	8	5	5	10	12
Swiss Cheese and Bacon Potatoes (p.71)	261	11	24	14	232	706	17	7	27	12	13	11	22	6
Volcano Potatoes (p. 65)	193	4	21	11	209	640	7	8	26	7	5	8	6	5
Whipped Turnips (p. 64)	159	3	11	12	234	443	4	11	35	7	6	4	10	4

Soups

	Calories	Protein (g)	Carbohydrate (g)	Fat (g)	Sodium (mg)	Potassium (mg)	Protein	Vitamin A	Vitamin C	Thiamine	Riboflavin	Niacin	Calcium	Iron
Autumnfest Soup (p. 76)	189	5	16	13	471	619	8	17	17	13	8	13	11	7
Broccoli-Cheese Soup (p. 77)	335	15	12	26	455	467	23	40	78	7	21	11	40	6
Celery-Spinach Soup (p. 28)	79	6	5	3	505	394	9	39	13	3	7	9	14	7
Cheesy Mushroom Soup (p. 76)	327	6	8	31	394	293	9	24	3	5	19	13	9	6
Chilled Spinach Soup (p. 74)	168	8	11	10	428	603	12	81	20	6	19	10	21	10
Corkscrew Vegetable Soup (p. 28)	81	4	13	1	465	266	6	115	5	9	8	13	3	5
Corn and Squash Soup (p. 29)	173	9	34	2	502	781	14	9	22	16	7	19	6	12
Creamy Pea Soup (p. 76)	171	8	14	10	427	323	12	20	19	15	10	14	7	8
French Onion Soup (p. 26)	402	17	34	22	1168	452	26	14	18	17	15	15	39	12
Hearty Potato Soup (p. 77)	333	11	30	19	717	687	16	91	18	20	14	19	11	6
Jambalaya Soup (p. 29)	128	15	13	2	506	597	24	20	42	23	7	18	11	14
Minestrone (p. 83)	284	16	43	6	576	703	25	109	10	30	16	18	20	24
Oriental Chicken-Vegetable Soup (p. 28)	114	16	6	3	950	532	24	120	12	6	13	38	7	12
Vegetarian Chilli (p. 80)	411	22	37	20	1176	1203	35	50	113	29	21	39	33	27

Miscellaneous

	Calories	Protein (g)	Carbohydrate (g)	Fat (g)	Sodium (mg)	Potassium (mg)	Protein	Vitamin A	Vitamin C	Thiamine	Riboflavin	Niacin	Calcium	Iron
Cream Cheese Icing (p. 36)	164	1	22	8	80	14	1	7	0	0	1	0	1	1
Mustard Sauce (p. 101)	46	1	2	4	129	61	2	3	0	1	3	0	5	0
Sunshine Carrot Cake (p. 36)	328	4	47	14	145	129	7	144	4	11	8	6	6	8
Sweet and Sour Sauce (p. 106)	60	0	15	0	170	75	0	0	0	0	0	0	0	2
Whole Wheat-Courgette Bread (p. 37)	201	3	30	8	104	108	5	2	3	8	4	4	2	6